# THE WINGS
# OF THE DOVE

## A Play in Three Acts

by

CHRISTOPHER TAYLOR

From the novel by

HENRY JAMES

SAMUEL FRENCH

LONDON

SAMUEL FRENCH **LTD**
26 SOUTHAMPTON STREET, STRAND, LONDON
SAMUEL FRENCH **INC**
25 WEST 45TH STREET, NEW YORK
7623 SUNSET BOULEVARD, HOLLYWOOD
SAMUEL FRENCH (CANADA) **LTD**
27 GRENVILLE STREET, TORONTO
SAMUEL FRENCH (AUSTRALIA) **PTY LTD**
ELIZABETHAN THEATRE TRUST BUILDING
153 DOWLING STREET, SYDNEY

MADE AND PRINTED IN GREAT BRITAIN BY
LATIMER TREND AND CO. LTD, PLYMOUTH

MADE IN ENGLAND

# THE WINGS OF THE DOVE

Produced by John Gale and Frith Banbury in association with Alan
Kaplan at the Lyric Theatre, London, on the 3rd December 1963,
with the following cast of characters:

*(in the order of their appearance)*

| | |
|---|---|
| MILLY THEALE | *Susannah York* |
| SUSAN SHEPHERD | *Wendy Hiller* |
| MAUD LOWDER | *Elspeth March* |
| KATE CROY, her niece | *Gene Anderson* |
| PASQUALE, a gondolier | *Graham Corry* |
| LORD MARK | *Owen Holder* |
| GANASETA, a footman | *Michael Dawson* |
| MERTON DENVER | *James Donald* |
| MARIA, a housemaid | *Fiona Dempster* |

Directed by FRITH BANBURY

Décor by LOUDON SAINTHILL

## SYNOPSIS OF SCENES

*The action of the Play passes in a salon of the Palazzo Leporelli,
Venice, at present the residence of Milly Theale*

### ACT I

SCENE 1   An afternoon in mid-October 1900
SCENE 2   A week later. Evening

### ACT II

SCENE 1   Five days later. Morning
SCENE 2   Three weeks later. Afternoon

### ACT III

SCENE 1   Three days later. Evening
SCENE 2   An afternoon in late December

# ACT I

## SCENE 1

SCENE—*A salon of the Palazzo Leporelli, Venice. An afternoon in mid-October 1900.*

*The room is rich and elegant. The left half of the back wall consists of a large arch.* C *of the semicircular surround above this arch, up one step, double doors lead on to a landing and other parts of the house off* R. *The right half of the back wall consists of a massive marble fireplace. Down* R, *an impressive door leads to other parts of the house. Two high, alcoved windows* L, *with balconies outside, overlook the canal. In each window there is a long low stool. A large, ornate gilt mirror hangs on the wall below the windows and a small console table, with a statue on it, stands between them. There is a small console table* R *of the double doors and another console table, with a bust on it is against the right side of the arch. A similar bust stands upon a pedestal against the left side of the arch. The fireplace has a club fender. On the mantelpiece stands a heavy marble clock and two Baroque figures. Above the mantelpiece hangs a dark, heavy tapestry. A bell-rope hangs* R *of the fireplace. An ornate desk with a chair above it, stands* L, *facing down* L. *A folding blotter and a heavy inkstand are on the desk. A high-back wing-chair stands* L *of the fireplace, facing down* RC, *with a draped oval table* R *of it.* R *of the fireplace is a chaise-longue, its head pointing to the up* R *corner of the room and its foot down* RC. *A small stool stands down* R, *below the door, and a small upright chair is down* L. *On the landing, outside the double doors, is a pedestal with a marble bust on it. At night the room is lit by candelabra and oil-lamps, brought in as required.*

*When the* CURTAIN *rises,* MILLY THEALE *is seated on the stool at the downstage window, one leaf of which is open, looking down at the canal. She is an American, aged twenty-three. Her skin is very pale. She is dressed in black, relieved only by a long, double rope of pearls. After a moment,* SUSAN SHEPHERD, *her friend, opens the double doors up* C, *unnoticed by* MILLY, *enters the room and stands just inside for a long, long moment, regarding Milly.* SUSAN *is in her early fifties and is slight in build. Her face is sweet and usually anxious.* MILLY *leans forward slightly to see something below. She experiences a moment of dizziness, sways from her seated position, then recovers. Suddenly sensing that someone else is in the room, she turns her head and, seeing Susan, smiles.* SUSAN *returns the smile and starts forward as if she had just entered the room.*

MILLY. Susan . . . !
SUSAN. Dearest . . .
MILLY. Had you been standing there for long?

SUSAN (*moving to* R *of the desk; with a comfortable, dissembling laugh*) Whatever makes you think that?

(MILLY *smiles and shrugs*)

MILLY.  Well ! ! We do know each other, don't we ?

SUSAN.  I should hope so, by now!

MILLY (*with a sense of wonder*) And yet, just a year ago—there I was alone in New York; there *you* were, alone in Boston. Neither of us knowing that the other even existed! Thank Heaven I met you, Susie.

SUSAN.  Thank Heaven *I* met *you*, my dear.

(MILLY *returns to the view*)

(*She picks up a "Baedeker" from the desk and flicks through a few pages*) This time I'll try St Mark's without my *Baedeker*. (*She replaces the book firmly on the desk*) Maud never opens hers; I doubt that Miss Croy owns one. And I sometimes think she'd rather I didn't read bits out aloud.

MILLY (*turning*) Oh . . . ?

SUSAN.  Well—people smile. "*La turista americana.*"

MILLY.  No!—here in Venice we're settlers, Susan! We're a settlement.

SUSAN (*taking in the room with a gesture*) "Settlement"?—a court!

MILLY (*delighted*) A court!

SUSAN (*leaning on the downstage edge of the desk*) And you are our princess.

MILLY.  Why, thanks!—but shouldn't I be queen? I mean, I am the last of the line—I'm the only one left. (*Remembering*) Oh, no, that wouldn't do. Kate and her aunt are English; they already have a queen.

SUSAN.  Be mine, then, Milly!

(MILLY *turns back to the window. Her face is suddenly grave again but she speaks lightly*)

MILLY.  For a while.

SUSAN (*with a worried little frown, but her voice agreeing gaily*) For a while. Until some prince . . . ! (*She regards Milly's back for a moment then picks up the "Baedeker" and crosses to the chaise*) I could read about St Mark's now, of course, until we're all ready to leave.

MILLY (*turning to Susan*) Would you think me quite abominable if I were to say . . .

SUSAN (*quickly; comfortably*) You'd rather just stay in again. (*She hopes for a denial*) Yes . . . ? (*She sits on the down* L *corner of the chaise*) This time I will, too.

MILLY (*rising and moving* C) No, please. We must remember— Kate and her aunt are staying with us now—they're our guests in Venice.

SUSAN.  Yes. (*She lays out the "Baedeker's" folded map* R *of her on the chaise*)

*To face page 2 — The Wings of the Dove*

*Photograph by Reg Wilson*

MILLY. And think of their hospitality while we were with them in London.

SUSAN. We must do our very best to repay it; I agree.

MILLY (*moving to* L *of Susan*) How I work you, Susie!

SUSAN. How you "work" me? Oh, yes—shamefully! Whirling me from Boston all the way to London! To London, to Maud Lowder—a friend I hadn't seen for a quarter century. Then—whirling me—(*she ticks off the entourage one by one on her fingers*) my friend and her niece all the way—(*her hands spread to take in the room*) to Venice!

MILLY (*moving above the wing-chair; nodding happily*) Mmm! I work dear Kate and Mrs Lowder too.

SUSAN (*returning to her "Baedeker" with feigned impatience*) Ohh . . . !

MILLY (*turning to Susan; carefully but without emphasis*) On the day we left London, when he came to see you alone, what was it, Susan, that Sir Luke Strett said to you?

SUSAN (*looking away; very startled*) The doctor? On the day we left?

MILLY. Yes. I don't mean while I was ill; of course the two of you *had* to put your heads together then.

SUSAN. Milly, dear—(*she rises and moves to* R *of the wing-chair*) we've no secrets from you.

MILLY. Then why did he want to see you alone?

SUSAN. You were with Mr Denver. How did you know?

(MILLY *crosses below the desk to the downstage window*)

MILLY (*as if satisfied and ready to drop the matter*) I only know now. I guessed.

SUSAN. But he told me nothing!

MILLY. Don't worry.

SUSAN. Dearest—are you—you're not in pain?

MILLY (*smiling*) Not the least little bit. (*She looks out of the window, puzzling*) But I wonder . . . (*She hesitates*)

SUSAN. Yes . . . ?

MILLY (*slowly and thoughtfully*) Sometimes I wonder . . . Well . . . If I shall have much of it.

SUSAN (*very distressed*) Milly!

MILLY (*turning, surprised by Susan's tone*) Much of life. Much of everything.

SUSAN (*relieved*) Oh. But you have!

MILLY (*pleasantly*) Not really.

SUSAN. More than almost anyone else.

MILLY (*reasonably*) I haven't everything.

SUSAN (*sufficiently reassured to be brisk*) You have me, at any rate. (*She moves down* RC) How can I help?

MILLY (*calmly*) Simply see me through. (*Almost gaily*) I'll be as easy for you as carrying a feather. (*She moves to* L *of Susan*) Don't worry. Please.

SUSAN. I'm not worrying, Milly.

(*They embrace lightly*)

MILLY (*as if concluding a bargain*) There—(*she kisses Susan's cheek*) see me through. It's understood. (*She moves to the doors up* C) And I won't ask again what he told you.

SUSAN. But he told me nothing dreadful! (*She moves above the wing-chair*) Nothing, nothing, nothing!

MILLY (*turning at the door; happily*) Of course not—there *is* nothing dreadful. You know what he told *me*. He told me to live.

(MILLY *exits up* C, *leaving the doors open.* SUSAN *moves down* C, *her hand to her mouth, fighting back tears*)

MAUD (*off*) Ah!—I'm coming to find Susan. Isn't she with you, dear?

(SUSAN *moves quickly to the fireplace*)

MILLY (*off*) She's in the—no, I can't say "saloon"—back home that's something so different.

MAUD (*off*) But when in Rome—or, rather Venice . . .

MILLY (*off*) You're right, of course. Susan's in the saloon. (*Her voice sounds farther off*) Oh! dear!—it does sound odd!

(MAUD LOWDER *enters up* C. *She is in her early fifties, an abundant, forceful and handsome matron. She wears an elaborate hat and cape and carries her handbag*)

SUSAN (*moving to* R *of the wing-chair*) Please, Maud. Shut the door.

(MAUD *looks at Susan with enquiring geniality*)

I'm sorry. I'm going to cry. (*She moves to the fireplace and stands with her back to Maud, in tears*)

MAUD. Susan . . . (*She closes the door*)

SUSAN. Make sure Milly isn't coming back. I'm sorry. Please be patient.

(MAUD *regards Susan for a moment then puts her bag on the table* R *of the arch*)

MAUD. Yes, dear, you cry. (*She adjusts her cape on her shoulders*) I shan't myself. (*She crosses to the mirror down* L *and looks in it*) But perhaps when Kate comes down, *she'll* participate. The poor vain thing is upstairs in her bedroom at the moment, pondering which hat will be most suitable for St Mark's. (*She turns and moves up* L *of the desk*) Oh, *there's* my writing-case! (*She picks up the case from the desk*) And that wretched parlour-maid swore she couldn't find it. (*She opens the case and takes out a letter*) Well, I must remember: twenty lira to be deducted from her tip when we depart. (*She stands between the desk and the desk chair*) I've a letter from Lady Danby——

(SUSAN *unsuccessfully stifles a sob*)

—so while you're occupied, my dear, I'll just knock off an answer.

(*She sits at the desk*) She's taken a house in Greece for the winter. Very original. The idea, that is—not the house, which, of course, I haven't seen. Although—she appears to be sounding me. And my niece. *Chiefly* my niece. (*Significantly*) Lord Mark is expected there.

(SUSAN *is not attending*)

(*She continues blandly*) You remember Lady Danby. She dined with us —twice—at Lancaster Gate while you and Milly were there.

SUSAN (*turning and sitting on the fender; through her tears*) Oh, Maud —I am so sorry!

MAUD. And rattled on about her plans for a literary salon. A literary salon, indeed! (*She brandishes Lady Danby's letter*) If you could see her spelling!

(KATE CROY *enters up* C. *She is aged twenty-six. She is beautiful and appears both proud and self-contained.* SUSAN *turns to hide her tears*)

(*She raises a restraining hand to Kate*) Not just now, Kate. We'll join you in a minute.

KATE (*to Susan*) Mrs Shepherd, did you know?—Milly says that, after all, she isn't coming with us.

MAUD (*immediately and firmly*) But of course she's coming with us. The only question is—are *you*?

(KATE *turns from regarding Susan's back to give Maud a glance of enquiry*)

(*With elaborately ill-concealed impatience*) Kate, Kate Croy: which hat —which hat? (*She sighs*) I make so many of your decisions. (*She motions to Kate to go*) Must I decide which hat as well?

KATE (*pleasantly, but with a slight ironic edge*) Thank you, Aunt Maud; no—not which hat . . .

(KATE *exits up* C, *closing the door behind her*)

MAUD (*turning to Susan*) You may continue now, my dear.

SUSAN. Oh, thank Heaven it wasn't Milly! I mustn't cry in front of her. Even if—but she won't, she won't!—Milly won't cry herself.

MAUD (*matter-of-factly*) I'm sure I hope Miss Theale will never have occasion. (*She commences to write*)

SUSAN. "The great thing—the only thing", he said, "is for her to be happy."

MAUD. By "he" you mean . . . ?

SUSAN (*with tearful impatience*) When he came to see me the day we left—(*She rises and leans across the table* C) oh, Maud, I *told* you! —the doctor!

MAUD (*putting down her pen; genially*) "Sir Luke." "Sir Luke Strett," Susan. And one of our very greatest men. You mustn't say, "the doctor".

SUSAN. But that's what we call our great man. (*She blows her nose and moves down* L *of the chaise*) Dr Buttrick, you know, of Boston. (*She sits on the downstage end of the chaise*)

MAUD. And if Sir Luke says that she must be happy, why must you cry so hard?

SUSAN. Only that if she can't be . . . !

MAUD (*pushing her letter aside*) "Can't?" She will. She shall. (*With a gusty sigh*) If only you'd trust me . . . !

SUSAN. I do!

MAUD (*as if repeating an oft-evaded question*) Then, Susan, what is wrong with her? Precisely what's her case?

SUSAN. I don't know, Maud. Nor does Milly. Now and then I've even wondered if Sir Luke quite knows himself. Of course, there's medicine, pills—and not wintering in London. She must stay put. (*She rises*) He'll visit her here.

MAUD (*impressed*) Will he!

SUSAN (*moving to the fireplace*) In two or three months.

MAUD. Sir Luke will come here! Well! That's proof of a huge interest; as well as a huge fee. (*She bristles*) But meanwhile, he ought not to scare us.

SUSAN (*rallying and moving down* RC) Does it scare us to help her be happy?

MAUD. It scares *me*—for the moment—but only because I must confess I don't quite understand. Miss Theale is rich; so am I, but, compared to her, I'm a pauper. Miss Theale is young, and I'm—well, look! Her charm is immense, mine isn't. But *I'm* not unhappy, so why should Miss Theale be? What's Sir Luke talking about?

SUSAN. Oh, you know.

MAUD (*doubting it*) Do I?

SUSAN. *I* do. (*She moves to the wing-chair, sits and leans across the left arm*) Dearest, we've both been married.

MAUD. So?

SUSAN. We've both, I trust, been in love.

MAUD (*snorting*) But not by doctor's order!

SUSAN (*smiling*) Still—it's nice to learn he thinks it's good for us.

MAUD. It strikes me, my dear, we've learned that much without him. But will it be good—*can* it be good—good enough, I mean, to cure whatever's wrong with Milly?

SUSAN. Sir Luke told her to live.

MAUD. Humph!

SUSAN. But she must *want* to, Maud.

MAUD (*with scornful impatience*) "Want to live!" *Doesn't* she?

SUSAN. She doesn't want to die. But why should he have told her to live, unless he saw—unless he feared . . .

MAUD. Tut, tut, tut.

SUSAN (*rising and crossing below the desk to the downstage window; on the verge of tears*) I've thought and thought of it.

MAUD. Tut, tut, tut, my dear. She's to live. Not a bad prescription.

SUSAN. The great thing, the only thing . . .

MAUD (*nodding impatiently*) "Is for her to be happy."

SUSAN. Those were his words.

MAUD (*archly*) And what were *yours*, dear? Did you tell him?

SUSAN (*turning to her*) Oh, Maud, I couldn't tell him *then*! Of course, *you* saw at once what Milly felt for Mr Denver.

MAUD (*smugly*) I knew in my bones.

SUSAN (*moving to L of Maud*) But it's only really since we've been *here* that I've had my impression.

MAUD. I knew in my bones she cared for him.

SUSAN. Poor, dear Milly . . . !

MAUD (*agreeing crossly*) It's provoking.

SUSAN. I mean, Maud—when it's so clear that Mr Denver loves your niece.

MAUD. Poor, dear Mr Denver, then!

SUSAN. But he longs for her——

MAUD (*snorting with grim amusement*) Huuh!

SUSAN (*crossing above Maud to R of her*)—so how—? (*She hesitates*)

MAUD. Yes . . . ? How . . . ?

SUSAN (*in despair*) How can he care for Milly?

MAUD (*firmly*) By being put in the way of it.

SUSAN (*crossing below the wing-chair to the right end of the fireplace*) For God's sake, then, *put* him there!

MAUD (*with a sly smile*) Well. We'll see. You know that I did what I could in London.

SUSAN (*moving to R of the table C*) You were magnificent.

MAUD. Magnificent? Of course I was—I *am*. (*Significantly*) But your little friend won't be, if she marries Merton Denver.

SUSAN. To marry the man one loves . . . (*A gentle but firm correction*) Oh, yes, Maud—that's magnificent. (*She smiles woefully*) But we're going fast . . . !

(MAUD *smiles slyly and rubs her hands together with self-satisfaction*)

MAUD. Even so, I'm ahead of you.

SUSAN (*startled*) Maud!

MAUD. Yes . . . ?

SUSAN. Just then! (*She leans across the table C. Excitedly*) Why—you might have been seventeen!

MAUD. *What?*

SUSAN. Years ago—

MAUD. Decades! Centuries!

SUSAN. Back in Vevey. At school. That's just what you were like when you had some wicked scheme. (*She moves below the table C*)

MAUD. God has been good. Dear Susan! God has been very good indeed. Somehow, after one's fifty, one doesn't make new friends. At my age, I wouldn't—I couldn't have made a new friend like you. But God's been keeping you for me in pink tissue paper and camphor——

SUSAN. Camphor—uggh! Lavender, please. (*She moves to the right end of the fireplace*)

MAUD.  And now, after all these many years, he's sent you back to me. Like a fairy tale.

SUSAN.  Milly waved her wand . . . !

MAUD.  Her magic wand; yes. And then, that she and Kate should have become such friends. It's beautiful. It's perfect. Or was. Until we came here. Sir Luke or no Sir Luke, I saw at once this wouldn't do.

SUSAN (*wondering what can be amiss with such a splendid dwelling*)  But, Maud, it's——

MAUD.  A circle of petticoats! Widows and orphans!

SUSAN (*laughing*)  Oh!

MAUD (*leaning forward on the desk*)  "Well," I thought, "he isn't much; in fact, he's nearly nothing; but every little helps." (*She turns complacently to Susan*)  You see, I *was* ahead of you.

SUSAN.  Yes . . . ?

MAUD.  He'll have had my letter early last week.

SUSAN.  Who, Maud?

MAUD (*impatiently*)  Merton Denver.

SUSAN.  No! (*She moves* RC, *very confused, but excited*)  But how?—why? —what did you say?

MAUD.  Simply that if he could see his way to spending a fortnight in Venice, I'd guarantee he'd find it to his—(*she smoothly corrects herself*)  he'd find a welcome here.

SUSAN (*euphoric*)  Oh, Maud! Maud, you *are* magnificent! (*She moves to* R *of the desk. Anxiously*)  His paper—will they let him come?

MAUD.  He'll come.

SUSAN (*eagerly*)  Yes, of course. One feels you have him in your hand.

MAUD.  That's your impression of him?

SUSAN.  Of *you*. You handle us all, my dear.

MAUD (*after a slight pause; looking away from Susan*)  I don't handle Kate.

SUSAN (*comfortably*)  Oh, I'm sure you— (*She breaks off with a gasp*)  You don't mean Kate *returns* his love?

(MAUD *turns, blinks and then stares at the question*)

(*She gropes frantically for an answer*)  Oh, no! (*She moves to* R *of the wing chair, arguing with herself*)  Of course, she's kind to him—and that's fine—I've so admired her—but I've never seen her so much as— (*She turns to Maud, insisting*)  Maud! Does Kate care for him?

(MAUD *meets* SUSAN'S *eyes and holds them*)

MAUD.  No. (*She rises, glances quickly at the doors up* C *then moves to* L *of the wing-chair*)  And you must deny it too. Positively and absolutely.

SUSAN (*after a stoic pause*)  To Milly, you mean.

MAUD.  No-one else will ask.

SUSAN.  Milly won't.

MAUD. Are you sure?

SUSAN. Yes. Luckily. I don't lie very well.

MAUD. I do, thank God. And, for that matter, so does Kate.

SUSAN. You mean, she won't tell Milly? But why—when they're so close? (*With sudden bewilderment*) Maud—why hasn't she already?

MAUD. My niece is thoroughly aware of my views for her. And aware, that so long as she's with me, she must agree with them. Well, my views do not provide any place at all for Mr Denver— much as, in a manner, I like him.

SUSAN (*a little aghast*) And because of that, she daren't speak even to Milly of what she feels? (*She moves and sits on the left side of the chaise. With wry humour*) And yet you say you don't handle her!

MAUD. She may agree with my views to Milly, to me—to the world, in fact. But alone . . . ? Or alone with him . . . ? Proud young women are sly. (*She moves and sits at the desk. Grimly*) And proud old women are—well, what I am. *If* she thinks she cares for him, she's wrong; she is mistaken.

SUSAN. Maud, it's a little frightening.

MAUD. Kate's frightened, certainly. Without me, she couldn't keep herself in cotton handkerchiefs. And she's not the girl for cotton. Oh, I've seen to that! I've seen to it that she's greedy.

SUSAN. She'll marry money, then?

MAUD. She'll marry a great man. Should he be poor, I'll help them.

SUSAN. Why not help Mr Denver?

MAUD. He isn't a great man.

SUSAN. Might he not become one?

MAUD. Never. Even the idea would not occur to him. He's charming, he's cultured and he's intelligent. As a literary journalist he'll have a nice career. With a little—not much—money; with a little—not much—power. And with that he'll be content.

SUSAN. Kate wouldn't be . . . ?

MAUD. *I* wouldn't. And for Kate that means plain cotton hand-kerchiefs. No, I've created her for something very different. Oh, yes!—she's my creation. On purpose to give interest to my declining years. And where's the interest in a marriage with Mr Merton Denver?

SUSAN. Her happiness, Maud. Aren't you interested in that?

MAUD (*pointedly*) In Milly's too.

SUSAN. Yes—Milly helps you.

MAUD (*bristling*) Helps me! I help *her*. (*She returns to her writing*)

SUSAN. Yes. Yes. But after all, we're only talking in the air.

(KATE *enters up* C. *She is dressed to go out*)

MAUD. Ah, Kate, my dear . . .

KATE. Milly still insists that she'd rather not come with us.

SUSAN. St Mark's! (*She rises and consults her fob-watch*) We asked for the gondola at three. I shan't be long. (*She tidies the map back into the* "*Baedeker*")

(KATE *moves to* L *of Susan*)

Gloves, purse and a hat. (*For Kate's benefit*) I'll leave my *Baedeker*.

KATE (*to Susan*) I tried—can't you persuade her?

SUSAN (*turning to Kate; gaily*) But Milly has months for St Mark's! And after the whirl, the rush in London—well, if I'm to persuade her, it must be to do what she's doing—to rest.

KATE (*troubled*) We don't want her ill again, certainly.

SUSAN (*crossing below Kate towards the desk; laughing away the idea*) Oh, my dear . . . !

KATE. Then it hasn't been at Sir Luke's suggestion . . . ?

SUSAN (*stopping and turning*) Should I understand?

KATE. Day after day—just staying in here.

MAUD. The sweet American thing! (*She takes in the room*) If I were paying for all of this, I shouldn't step out for one minute. (*She resumes her letter*)

(SUSAN *puts the "Baedeker" on the desk and moves above the wing-chair*)

SUSAN (*laughing incredulously*) "Sir Luke's suggestion?" No! (*With a quick rush of sympathy*) You've been worried. I wish you'd told me.

KATE. One can't tell her. She laughs.

SUSAN (*moving to the doors up* C; *contrite*) And so did I. I'm sorry. (*She turns*) Don't worry, though.

KATE. I won't.

(SUSAN *smiles and exits up* C, *closing the door behind her*)

(*After a pause*) She's very gravely ill. I'm certain.

MAUD (*flatly*) No, my dear. She's not. (*She tears the sheet from her pad, turns it over and continues with her writing*)

KATE (*after a glance at Maud*) Well . . . (*She dismisses the subject with a little shrug and moves to the right end of the fireplace*)

MAUD. I've a letter from Lady Danby. I'm just knocking off an answer.

KATE. I've had one, too.

MAUD (*writing*) Yes . . . ? That was excessive of her, surely.

KATE. From Mr Denver.

MAUD (*putting down her pen*) Oh.

(MAUD *turns slowly in her chair to meet* KATE's *eyes. For a moment each waits for the other to break the silence*)

KATE. Scarcely a letter, in point of fact. He wrote in some haste.

MAUD (*nodding*) Before leaving.

KATE. Before arriving, say.

MAUD. He's very good. Very good indeed. I do like him. (*With a gusty sigh*) What a nuisance!

(KATE *gives Maud a coolly quizzical look*)

My liking him so, the poor young man. When he cares for you—too much.

KATE (*with a fleeting, ironic smile*) Too much?

MAUD (*unctuously*) And I don't want you worried.

KATE (*impersonally polite*) Thank you, Aunt Maud, but—

MAUD (*with a genial wave*) I *know*, my dear—you, in turn, don't want *me* worried. And so, if he—privately—well, besets you, you keep it to yourself. (*Firmly*) But he shan't. (*She forestalls an imaginary objection*) No, no—he shan't—I promise. *I* suggested he come. It's my responsibility.

(KATE *gives another fleeting ironic smile, and a nod of acquiescence*)

KATE. May I know, then, *why* you suggested he come?

MAUD (*impatiently returning to her letter*) I told you. Because I like him.

KATE. *Do* you?

MAUD (*casually*) Oh, dear, yes. Don't you?

(*There is a slight pause*)

KATE (*turning to the fireplace*) You're quite wonderful, Aunt Maud.

MAUD. So Susan has been insisting. (*She checks her letter*) Lady Danby expects Lord Mark. She suggests that we come for November. I think that perhaps in a fortnight or so . . . (*She writes*)

KATE (*emphatically*) No.

(MAUD *stops writing and lifts her head, but does not look at Kate*)
Milly is *not* well.

MAUD (*writing*) If—if not, she will be by then.

KATE (*firmly*) No. Please don't commit us.

MAUD (*calmly putting down her pen and tearing the sheet across*) Very good. I'll begin again. (*She puts the torn pieces in her writing-case and rises*) But it is not my wish—(*she moves to the table* R *of the arch and picks up her handbag*) nor, I'm sure is it yours—to disappoint Lord Mark.

(SUSAN *enters up* C, *leaving both doors open. She wears her hat and cape and carries her handbag and gloves*)

SUSAN (*moving to* L *of Maud*) Are we ready?

MAUD. Susan, have you your parasol? (*She takes her gloves from her handbag*)

(PASQUALE, *a gondolier on Milly's staff, enters up* C *and stands* L *of the doors*)

SUSAN (*putting on her gloves*) Why, no. I thought rather a coat . . .

MAUD. Yes, I dare say . . . (*She turns and sees Pasquale. Pleased and surprised*) Oh, are you taking us—? (*To Susan*) What *is* his name?

SUSAN (*turning to Pasquale*) Pasquale! We *are* honoured.

PASQUALE. *Scusi, signora, ma la signorina Theale viene con lei?*

SUSAN. No, Pasquale, *non oggi.* Miss Theale is staying here.

PASQUALE. *Allora—la conduce Italo.* (*With a gesture towards the door*) *Vuol uscire adesso?*

SUSAN. *Sì, sì.* (*To Maud*) Italo's taking us.

MAUD. Italo again! What's the matter with *this* one?

SUSAN   We are ready?

MAUD (*to Kate*) Come along, dear. (*moving to the doors up* C) Will we have time for a look-in at that lace shop in the Piazza? Kate has been very good. (*She smiles at Kate*) I want to buy her something.

(MAUD *exits up* C)

KATE (*gesturing to Susan that she should precede her through the doors*) Oh, I think St Mark's will be enough to occupy us.

SUSAN (*moving to the doors*) A lace shop? In the Piazza San Marco? I don't remember, dear.

(SUSAN *exits up* C.
KATE *follows her off*)

MAUD (*off*) Yes. You know the—what are they called?—galleries, arcades.

SUSAN (*off*) "*Loggia*," dear.

MAUD (*off*) "*Loggia*." In one of *them*.

(PASQUALE *closes the doors, crosses hurriedly to the door down* R, *opens it and speaks to someone outside*)

PASQUALE.   *Le signore sono uscite, signore.*

LORD MARK (*off down* R; *sharply*) You don't mean that Miss Theale is with them?

PASQUALE.   No, *signore*. (*He steps aside*)

(LORD MARK *enters down* R. *He is in his late thirties. He is a man of rather colourless appearance, but has an air of immense, quiet authority. He carries his hat*)

LORD MARK.   Good. (*He crosses to the foot of the chaise*)

PASQUALE (*moving to* R *of Lord Mark*) *Se ha la bonta d'aspettar qui, signore, vado a chiedere alla Signorina Theale se puo riceverla.*

LORD MARK (*taking out his wallet and extracting a lira note*) *Grazie.* And thank you for—well, you understand, I've so very little time; and I'd have felt a brute—interrupting their excursion. (*He holds out the note*) *Grazie.*

PASQUALE (*taking and pocketing the note*) *Vado a cercare la signorina* Theale.

(PASQUALE *exits down* R, *closing the door behind him.* LORD MARK *surveys the room briefly and dispassionately. He crosses the room, but without curiosity, places his hat on the right end of the desk, chooses the wing-chair and sits. He is still for some moments, thinking and waiting.*

MILLY *enters up* C, *carrying a book. She turns and closes the door.* LORD MARK *rises and stands* R *of the wing-chair. As* MILLY *turns from the door, believing the room to be empty, she sees Lord Mark*)

MILLY (*startled*) Oh!

LORD MARK (*with a step towards her*) Miss Theale . . .

MILLY (*laughing and gasping*)  Oh, goodness! I've never been so startled!

LORD MARK (*moving to her*)  I'm so very sorry. Didn't your man-servant . . . ?

MILLY (*offering her hand*)  Lord Mark! Lord Mark, of all people!

(LORD MARK *takes her hand. As his left hand comes up to cover it,* MILLY *disengages and continues with great excitement*)

When did you—? Where are the others? Why didn't they tell me you were here?

LORD MARK.  A rather splendid fellow in a sash went to——

MILLY.  Pasquale, I should think. But Kate and Mrs Lowder . . . ?

LORD MARK.  I gather I missed them. By minutes.

MILLY.  Oh, dear! Of course! They've gone off to St Mark's with Susan. (*She moves to the upstage window and looks down*) Won't Kate be happy that you're here! I can't wait to see her face. Nor can you, can you! (*She moves to* L *of him*) Why don't you catch them up?

LORD MARK.  Why, no, I——

MILLY.  I'll lend you Pasquale. (*She crosses below Lord Mark to the bell-rope* R *of the fireplace*)

LORD MARK (*moving to* L *of the wing-chair*)  It's a question of time. I——

MILLY.  He seems to have appointed himself my personal gon-dolier. (*She reaches for the bell-rope*) But, you see, I don't go about and so——

LORD MARK (*almost sharply*)  No—please don't!

(MILLY *turns unwillingly from the bell-rope*)

(*He moves to her. More gently*) But why? Why don't you go about?

(MILLY *is uneasy as she senses the reason for Lord Mark's disinclina-tion to leave*)

MILLY.  I go about here—just here. It suits me so.

LORD MARK.  Do you mean that you're not well?

(PASQUALE *enters up* C. *For the moment, he only sees Lord Mark and moves up* L *of the desk chair*)

PASQUALE.  *Mi dispiace, Signore, ma non posso . . .*

(LORD MARK *turns to Pasquale and takes a step up* C)

MILLY (*quickly*)  Pasquale!

PASQUALE (*seeing Milly*)  Ah, Signorina!

MILLY (*crossing quickly to Pasquale*)  Now, I want you to take Lord Mark and catch up with the other gondola.

LORD MARK (*moving to* R *of Milly*)  I'm afraid that——

MILLY.  They've gone to St Mark's.

LORD MARK.  —I've less than an hour, I'm *en route* for Greece. And it's you I want to see.

MILLY (*turning to Lord Mark*)  But, please—I can't be so selfish.

B

LORD MARK. It's a question of time—quite simply. (*He turns away above the wing-chair*)

MILLY (*turning to Pasquale*) Then, Pasquale—quick, go and catch up with them. Tell the ladies Lord Mark is here. Lord Mark. You understand?

PASQUALE. *Va bene.* I understand.

(PASQUALE, *with a malicious smile for Lord Mark's benefit, exits up* C, *closing the door behind him*)

MILLY. I hope he does. (*She puts her book on the left end of the desk*) "Lord Mark," "*St* Mark's"—it might be a bit confusing. Of course, not if he knew you— (*She catches herself with a laugh*) Oh—I didn't mean . . . !

(*There is a slight pause.* LORD MARK *remains still, quietly smiling and* MILLY *moves to the downstage window and looks down*)

If you did only miss them by minutes, they might still be in sight. Our view is marvellous, don't you think?

(LORD MARK *smiles*)

Don't you like my hired palazzo?

(LORD MARK *nods*)

I never tire of it.

LORD MARK (*moving down* R *of the desk*) But Venice itself . . . ! You *are* well?

MILLY. For me, this is all of Venice.

LORD MARK (*teasing*) You'd like—for ever—to live just here?

MILLY (*smiling*) For ever and ever.

LORD MARK (*laughing*) No—it's not good enough for *that* !

(LORD MARK's *laughter reassures* MILLY *and she relaxes*)

MILLY. I adore it.

LORD MARK. For a while. "A hired palazzo."

MILLY (*wandering up* C *then to* R *of the chaise*) I've wondered if they'd sell . . .

LORD MARK (*turning as Milly moves above him*) For money. (*He moves down* L *of the desk*) For money enough.

MILLY. I've wondered. I may try.

LORD MARK (*with a step towards her; with an amused protest*) Miss Theale!

MILLY (*clasping her hands together*) And if I do get it, oh, then I'll cling to it. (*Half to herself*) It will be my life—paid for—bought. (*To Lord Mark, with dissembling irony*) It will be my great gilded shell.

LORD MARK (*moving* C) With you the walnut?

MILLY (*happily*) Rattling around. Wasted, shrunken, wizened.

LORD MARK. Oh, but we can do better.

MILLY (*shaking her head*) No. London has too many—thicknesses, layers. It——

LORD MARK (*firmly*) I can do better, I mean.

MILLY (*lightly mocking, but again apprehensive*) Than Mrs Lowder?
—than Miss Croy?—Than Mrs Shepherd, even?

LORD MARK (*parenthetically*) Oh, Mrs Shepherd's all right. (*Decisively*) But better than her, even—certainly, if you'll have confidence.

MILLY. In you, Lord Mark? I have. Please don't undermine it.

LORD MARK (*moving to her; with true concern*) Are you really—troubled?

MILLY (*turning away*) Don't say—don't try to say anything.

LORD MARK (*quickly*) Look here, you know, that's monstrous. If one can't ask you, as a friend, what one so wants to——

MILLY (*turning and cutting in with perceptible hardness*) What is it you want to know?

LORD MARK (*flushing*) Can I see you suffer and not say a word?

MILLY. You won't see me suffer. Don't be afraid. I shan't be a public nuisance. (*She looks around the room. Softer*) That's why I want this.

LORD MARK (*very troubled*) Your friends—do they know?

MILLY (*turning to him; hard and peremptory*) What? *You* don't!

(*There is a pause. They face each other then* MILLY *relaxes and sits on the up* L *side of the chaise*)

(*Kindly*) I'm sorry. (*Dispassionately*) I'm badly ill.

LORD MARK. And you don't do anything?

MILLY. I do everything. Everything's this. (*She smiles*) One can't do more than live.

LORD MARK. Than live in the right way. *Do* you? Haven't you advice?

MILLY. The best, and I obey it. I live. As I said, one can't do more.

LORD MARK (*turning away down* C; *impatiently*) Oh, "live"!

MILLY (*smiling*) Yes. For me that's—well, I shan't miss everything.

LORD MARK (*turning to her*) Why anything?

MILLY (*with a little shrug*) Oh . . .

LORD MARK (*moving to* L *of her*) Miss Theale, you believe in advice. Take mine, then.

MILLY. But I've——

LORD MARK. I know what you need.

MILLY (*a gentle but firm warning*) I think I need not to be worried.

LORD MARK. You need to be adored.

MILLY. Lord Mark . . .

LORD MARK. Nothing would worry you less. I mean, as I shall do it. Let me——

MILLY. No.

LORD MARK. Let me try.

MILLY (*with a sudden smile*) Would you have to try so hard?

LORD MARK. What? (*Deflated*) Why, no. Of course not. (*He moves above the chaise. Persistently*) It's true, you know, and I don't care a hang for your trying to freeze me up. (*He moves to* R *of the chaise. With more confidence*) How did I know that you were troubled—when no-one else has guessed? Love makes out things like that, but——

MILLY (*cutting in; with a smile*) Isn't love supposed to be blind?

LORD MARK. To faults, but not to beauty.

MILLY. Then, are my private worries, which I'm ashamed to have let you glimpse—(*with a certain edge*) are they my beauty?

(LORD MARK, *thrown out of his stride, crosses below the chaise to* C)

LORD MARK. That's absurd!—how could they be?—I ask you!

MILLY (*looking away; vaguely*) Ohh—to a man who cared less for me than for . . . (*She trails off the sentence with a little gesture*)

LORD MARK (*turning to her; expressionless*) Than for . . . ?

(MILLY, *surprised that Lord Mark should insist on her completing the implication, faces him*)

MILLY. All that I possess.

LORD MARK (*with an ironic but compassionate smile*) But that's so little—almost nothing—while you still lack what you need most. (*He moves to her and raises his hand to her shoulder*) You need somebody of your own.

MILLY. If so, need he be *you?*

(LORD MARK *withdraws his hand, turns and moves below the desk.* MILLY, *seeing that* LORD MARK *knows he has been finally rebuffed, rises and moves* C)

(*More gently*) Dear Lord Mark, you know, I don't think you're doing right. Nor I, in listening to you—except, I'm *not* listening. You shouldn't have come to see just *me*. You've older friends, and better.

LORD MARK (*picking up his hat and turning to Milly*) Kate Croy?

MILLY. It isn't as if one's turning you out into the cold world. For *you*, there'll never be one.

LORD MARK (*pleasantly*) I'm to marry Kate? (*Dryly*) Ever so kind of you to see such opportunities for me.

MILLY. She's the cleverest, handsomest——

LORD MARK. And for the asking?

MILLY (*gaily*) Try!

(*There is a slight pause*)

LORD MARK (*with a step towards her*) Then—don't you really *know?*

MILLY (*turning away; her face clouding slightly*) I "know" that a particular person's in love with her, yes.

LORD MARK. And that she's in love with a "particular person".

MILLY. Oh!—I beg your pardon. You're mistaken

LORD MARK. Am I?

MILLY. Yes.

LORD MARK (*his stare becoming a smile*) Are you so very, *very* sure?

MILLY (*with complete conviction*) As sure as I can be.

LORD MARK. That means, from Kate herself?

(MILLY *nods*)

She's thinking of no-one?

MILLY. Not of him. (*She sees he is still unconvinced*) I have her word.

LORD MARK (*moving to* L *of her*) Her word. Indeed. And what is that?

MILLY (*a sharp rebuke*) Lord Mark! (*She moves away to the foot of the chaise, relents and turns to him*) We're very close, and so—without prying, naturally Kate tells me certain things.

LORD MARK (*smiling*) And this "certain thing" is one of them.

MILLY (*losing patience*) She has left no doubt whatever of her being free.

LORD MARK (*moving to her*) And so of your being. For him, at least. Well . . . !

(MILLY, *after what is almost a glare at him, crosses towards the doors up* C)

MILLY. Pasquale seems to have failed, but I hope that you can wait. If you'll excuse me, now, I——

(GANASETA, *the footman, opens both doors up* C *and enters. He has a silver salver with a visiting card on it. He stands* L *of the doors*)

Oh, Ganaseta, have the ladies returned? Did Pasquale catch them up?

GANASETA. *Permesso, Signorina.* (*He offers the card on the salver*)

MILLY. Yes? (*She takes the card, reads it, then is motionless for a moment before instructing Ganaseta*)

(LORD MARK *moves to* R *of the wing-chair*)

I'll see him with pleasure.

(GANASETA *bows and exits up* C, *leaving the doors open*)

(*She moves to* R *of the arch. Hushed, puzzled, but happy, she looks at Lord Mark*) Mr Merton Denver.

LORD MARK (*crossing below Milly to the doors up* C) Oh.

MILLY. But you'll wait . . . ?

LORD MARK (*turning; a cool apology*) Unfortunately. Thank you for receiving me.

(LORD MARK *exits up* C. MILLY *stands for a moment in happy expectation, then runs to the mirror down* L, *looks in it and pinches her cheeks*)

SUSAN (*off up* C) Lord Mark! You *are* here! Why, when Pasquale caught us up in mid-stream we couldn't believe our ears. Excuse me—Mrs Lowder and Kate are just coming up—I must find Milly.

(SUSAN *enters very excitedly up* C *and moves to* R *of the desk.* MILLY *turns hastily from the mirror*)

Milly—do you know who's here?

MILLY (*moving below the left end of the desk*)  Yes; Mr Denver, Susan.

SUSAN (*beaming*)  Well . . . !

MILLY.  Poor man. I hope they won't be annoyed.

SUSAN (*moving down* LC; *faltering*)  Oh—you mean, because—? (*Firmly reassuring*) Kate Croy can take care of Kate Croy. And you know how little Maud makes of it. (*She beams, removes her gloves and moves above Milly to* L *of the desk*) Besides, we welcome him.

MILLY (*showing her delight*)  Of course!

> (MAUD *enters up* C *and stands above the wing-chair.*
> MERTON DENVER *follows her on. He is in his early thirties. He is engaging, with rather rumpled good looks*)

MAUD.  I've left my niece to dispose of Lord Mark. And here is someone nicer.

MERTON (*moving to* R *of the desk and holding out his hand*)  Miss Theale.

MILLY (*moving to Merton and shaking hands*)  Benevenuto a Venezia.

MERTON.  You're a native already.

MILLY (*very pleased*)  Oh . . . !

SUSAN (*moving to* L *of Milly*)  We do so hope you haven't come for a mere few foolish days.

MILLY.  You'll stay with us, Mr Denver?

MERTON.  Stay . . . ?

MILLY.  We've I can't tell you how many beds.

MAUD (*with a guffaw*)  Oh, you subtle thing!

MERTON.  Thank you, but I found an hotel.

> (KATE *enters down* R, *closes the door and goes to the fireplace. She still wears her hat and gloves*)

MILLY.  You can dine with us, though?

MERTON.  Thank you. Yes.

MILLY.  Tonight?

> (MERTON *smiles and nods*)

Every night?

> (MERTON *continues to smile*)

Oh, good. I'm glad. (*She crosses below Merton to Kate*) Kate—Mr Denver's to dine with us! What did we order? (*Flushed and happily anxious, she crosses below Kate to the head of the chaise*) I must see. And tell them. We might have some music afterwards! Susan—do you think you could help me?

SUSAN (*crossing down* R)  Yes, dear . . . ?

MILLY.  With your Italian. (*To Merton*) I *am* learning, though.

> (MERTON *smiles and moves to* L *of the desk.*
> SUSAN *exits down* R)

(*She moves to the door down* R *and turns*)  Well, if you'll . . .

MAUD (*genially waving her out*)  Of course, my dear.

MILLY.  We shan't be long.

(MILLY *exits down* R, *closing the door behind her*)

MAUD.  No. (*She moves to the desk, picks up her writing-case and throws a glance of grimly ironic amusement at Merton and Kate*) No, nor shall I. But in view of Lord Mark's so fleeting visit—(*to Kate*) I must think hard about how to answer Lady Danby, mustn't I? (*She moves to the doors up* C *and turns to Merton as if with an afterthought. Arch and sugary*) While you're in Venice, don't too much neglect our little American friend.

(MAUD, *smiling sweetly, exits up* C, *closing the doors behind her*)

MERTON (*with a step below the desk*)  She's playing with us!

KATE.  Yes. (*She moves down* RC *a little*) But we're a strong team, you and I.

MERTON.  When she sent for me, I thought perhaps—you'd persuaded her.

(KATE *shakes her head*)

Then, for God's sake, leave her. Marry me.

KATE.  But we'd have nothing.

MERTON.  More—much more than we have now.

KATE (*with a step or two towards him*)  Wait for me. Give me time. I see my way. Don't spoil it.

MERTON.  Do you love me?

KATE.  I see my way. (*She takes another step nearer to him*) I have a plan.

MERTON.  *Do you love me?*

KATE (*laughing*)  Yes.

MERTON *and* KATE *move to each other as*—

*the* CURTAIN *falls*

## SCENE 2

SCENE—*The same. A week later. Evening.*

*When the* CURTAIN *rises, the window curtains are closed. Two tall, ornate, six-branch standard candelabra, with six tall candles and shades each, have been set, one* L *of the doors up* C *and one* R *of the fireplace. The one* L *of the doors has all the candles lit. The other,* R *of the fireplace, has only three candles lit. An oil-lamp has been lit and set on the table between the windows. The oil-lamp on the table* R *of the wing-chair is also lit.* GANASETA *is* R *of the fireplace, lighting with a taper the three remaining candles of the candelabrum.* SUSAN *is seated in the wing-chair working at some embroidery. Her sewing-bag is on the table* R *of her chair.* GANASETA *finishes and blows out the taper.*

Susan (*after a glance at both candelabra*) That looks very nice, Ganaseta.

Ganaseta (*not understanding*) Signora?

Susan. *Quello sta molto bene.*

Ganaseta. *Si, signora. Grazie.* (*He crosses to the desk and picks up a box of candles*)

Susan. *Adesso farete la sala di musica, vero?*

Ganaseta. *Va bene, signora.* (*He crosses to the door down* R)

(Milly *enters up* c, *half dragging and half carrying another candelabrum, taller than she herself, matching those already in the room, but without candles or shades*)

Milly. Oh, Ganaseta—wait!

Ganaseta (*stopping and turning*) Signorina! (*He moves quickly up* c, *puts the box of candles on the table* R *of the arch, relieves Milly of her burden and closes the doors*)

Susan (*rising in concern*) Milly! What *are* you up to?

Milly (*to Ganaseta*) We'll need more candles for this one. (*She points down* L) I thought it might stand over there.

Susan. *Vicino alla finestra*, Ganeseta.

(Ganaseta *carries the candelabrum down* L)

Really, Milly—these last few days!

Milly (*picking up the box of candles and moving below the desk*) It's only wood; it's light. (*She checks the candles in the box*) Oh, good, we still have quite a lot. (*To Ganaseta, indicating with the box*) May *I* do this one, Ganaseta?

(Ganaseta, *assuming that Milly is pantomiming instructions, reaches for the box*)

Ganaseta. *Si, si, lo faro.*

Milly (*handing the box to Ganaseta; disappointed*) Oh. All right, then.

Susan (*moving down* c) Ganaseta!

Ganaseta (*crossing to Susan*) Signora?

Susan. *Lo vuol far da se.*

Ganaseta (*turning and offering the box to Milly*) Signorina?

Milly (*moving to* L *of Ganaseta*) Oh, thanks, Ganaseta. (*She takes two candles from the box, goes to the candelabra down* L *and puts the candles in the sconces*)

(Ganaseta *puts the box on the right end of the desk and crosses to the door down* R)

(*She calls to Ganaseta*) *Grazie!*

Ganaseta. *Prego.*

(Ganaseta, *bewildered, exits down* R)

Susan. Well, when you pick up the Leporelli's piano and carry *it* downstairs, I hope——

MILLY (*protesting happily*) Susie!—it wasn't heavy! (*She illustrates by lifting the candelabra*) Look!

SUSAN (*hiding her eyes with mock horror*) I'd better see to Ganaseta.

(MILLY *collects three candles from the box*)

(*Scolding fondly*) You're not—and it's vain to pretend—(*she tidies her embroidery, etc., into the bag*) you're not yet as sound and strong as I insist you must be.

MILLY (*moving down* L) The day I look *that* sound and strong, I shall take leave of you sweetly for ever. (*She puts the candles in the sconces*)

SUSAN. Then, at least, we'll know where we are!

MILLY. Where I am? Oh. (*She glances to Heaven and to the floor*) Up or down?

SUSAN (*pretending to consider*) Hmmm. (*Dryly*) Somewhere in between.

MILLY. That will do; that's where I am right now. (*She moves below the desk*) Please. (*Cheerfully*) I know how I look: even at my most fetching—(*she looks "fetching"*) fit for nothing much gayer than a handsome cemetery. (*She takes one candle from the box*)

SUSAN (*with mock exasperation*) Ohh!

MILLY. I know how I look! (*Sincerely*) And I know how I feel. (*She moves to Susan*) Truly, Susan, I'm *well*.

SUSAN. You must not take these risks, though.

MILLY. Why not? Risk everything!

SUSAN (*bridling happily*) Very well, then, I'll prepare for the worst—of sorrow and of sin. (*She draws the strings of her sewing-bag smartly together*)

(KATE *enters down* R, *leaving the door open. She is dressed for dinner*)

MILLY (*almost dancing to the candelabrum down* L) Oh, it's a stupendous world, and everyone—yes, everyone . . . ! (*She turns and breaks off as she sees Kate*)

KATE. Everyone what, Milly?

' MILLY (*suddenly grave*) Everyone wants to be so kind.

SUSAN (*moving to the head of the chaise*) "Kind," did you say?

MILLY. Doesn't Kate look handsome?

SUSAN (*inspecting Kate*) Those are the garnets Maud chose for you.

KATE (*touching one of her ear-rings*) Yes—last week.

SUSAN (*without enthusiasm*) Very nice. But what can the time be! (*She looks at her fob watch and crosses above Kate to the door down* R) We must hurry.

(SUSAN *exits down* R)

MILLY (*calling after Susan*) Mr Denver won't be back till eight.

(SUSAN *closes the door behind her*)

KATE (*moving and sitting on the upstage left end of the chaise*) I was bored, so I thought, "I'll take hours to dress." But didn't. *Who* is kind?

MILLY (*placing the last candle in its sconce*) I said everyone.

KATE. Everyone's no-one. Who in particular?

MILLY. You are.

KATE. Thank you. And who else?

MILLY (*sincerely*) No, please—don't make fun of me. (*She moves below the desk*)

KATE. But why choose to say he's kind?

MILLY. The past week. Every afternoon. And, lately, mornings too. Sitting in here or strolling through the rooms alone with me. Well—it can't be what he'd hoped.

KATE. Oh, dear—I must confess I thought you rather cared for him! And instead, here you've been . . . (*Commiserating*) Oh, darling Milly!—such a trial!

MILLY (*bewildered*) What . . . ?

KATE. Endlessly, patiently, pleasantly—! (*Palms held up and out, she mimes keeping someone at his distance*)

MILLY (*crossing to Kate; hastily correcting*) Oh, no!—it's Mr Denver who's patient and pleasant, Kate.

KATE (*pretending not to understand*) Mr Denver?

MILLY. Yes—and *kind*. Because he must have hoped . . . (*She hesitates*)

(KATE *gives her a puzzled look of enquiry*)

When he came here . . .

KATE. Yes . . . ?

MILLY. Hoped for *you*.

(KATE *laughs*)

Or something more of you.

(KATE *laughs again*)

And something less of me.

(KATE *rocks with laughter, rises, moves to Milly and kisses her cheek*)

KATE. Oh, you dear! You darling! Except, of course, that it would be a dreadful, tiresome nuisance, it would be so flattering I almost wish it true.

MILLY. But isn't it? Surely.

KATE. A year ago it might have been. Well—even less than that, perhaps. But, as you know—I've told you—I could never care for him.

MILLY. He for you, though.

KATE (*moving to the fireplace; dismissing the idea*) Time's taken care of that. Time and my— (*She repeats her "keeping-someone-at-his-distance" mime*) To say nothing of a certain young American's weird charms.

MILLY (*moving hurriedly to* L *of Kate; excitedly*) Do you think so—really?

KATE (*lightly*) Yes, I'm sure of it.

MILLY (*sitting on the fender; with a happy sigh*) Oh . . . !

KATE (*sitting* R *of Milly on the fender; smiling*) What now?

MILLY. Nothing. Kate . . . !

KATE (*with very affectionate irony*) "It's a stupendous world . . ."

MILLY (*happily*) "And everyone, yes, everyone——" (*She stops and screws up her face*)

KATE. "Wants to be so kind."

MILLY. No. I want some other word this time. "Kind" is rather —well, you know, there's not much *room* in it.

(SUSAN *enters up* C)

SUSAN (*moving up* L *of the wing-chair*) I told you to hurry, didn't I? See—we've both been caught.

(MERTON *enters up* C *and stands* R *of the desk chair. He wears evening dress.* MILLY *and* KATE *rise.*

GANASETA *enters up* C, *carrying a lighted oil-lamp, puts it on the table* R *of the doors up* C, *and exits*)

MILLY (*crossing quickly to the candelabrum down* L) And I wanted the room to be—oh, dear!

SUSAN (*moving and collecting the box of candles from the desk*) The room is fine.

KATE (*moving and sitting in the wing-chair*) It would seem the Leporellis were content with lamps.

MILLY (*abandoning the candelabrum down* L) This one tomorrow night, then.

SUSAN (*to Merton*) We grow more splendid all the time. (*She puts the box on the table* R *of the arch*)

MERTON. But in a true Venetian style. (*To Milly*) You've made me quite discontented, you know, with my hotel, which is anything —everything other than Venetian: German porters, Swiss clerks——

KATE (*cutting in; dryly*) French maids and English guests.

(GANASETA *enters up* C, *carrying a lighted oil-lamp. He places the lamp on the right end of the mantelpiece, then exits down* R, *closing the door behind him*)

MERTON (*tapping his chest*) Well, as for me, no longer.

MILLY (*moving to* L *of the desk; unable to hide her distress*) You're not leaving, then . . . !

MERTON. I've left.

SUSAN (*moving to* L *of the wing-chair; with concern*) But no—not Venice, Mr Denver.

MERTON (*to Milly*) I've done what you have done. Oh!—on a very humble scale. I'd noticed one or two houses—on the other side, much further down the Grand Canal—with white strips of paper pasted to their shutters. And this afternoon I asked Pasquale what they signified. An invitation, as he put it. To prospective tenants.

MILLY. Then you've become a settler too!

MERTON. And equally authentic. Indeed, more so, perhaps.

MILLY. Candle-light—*just* candle-light?

MERTON (*trying to remember*) Wait—no, there is a lamp! Two rooms: crooked, sloping, just above the water—you seem to hear it gurgling underneath your feet. Rickety chairs with seats of plush—old plush, very old: so old, in fact, it's bald. The rooms and everything in them are—well, like the old *padrona* who answered when I rang.

KATE. Poor woman—she's bald too, then?

MILLY (*laughing*) Kate . . . !

(SUSAN *does not join in the laughter, but gives Kate a cold look*)

MERTON (*moving* R *of the desk; to Kate*) No, but genial, shabby, ancient—and, from her cap to the tip of her boot, pure Venetian rococo. (*He moves down* C *and turns to Milly*) Oh, *this* is a thousand and one grand things, but seeing rooms like mine——

MILLY. Enough! Mr Denver, it is your plain duty to invite me —tomorrow or the next day, some day very soon—to tea.

SUSAN⎱ (*together*) ⎰(*Delighted and astonished*) Oh, yes!
KATE ⎰         ⎱(*Delighted*) You must!

MILLY. And Susan, too.

MERTON. But, Miss Theale, can it be wise for you to——

(KATE *rises and speaks rather louder than she had intended, to prevent a demur*)

KATE. Milly—! (*She stops, at a brief loss for something to say*) Would you like me to—shall I come with you while you dress?

(SUSAN *crosses quickly to the door down* R)

MILLY. Oh. (*She signals with a look that Merton must not be abandoned*) Well, when your aunt comes down, perhaps. (*She crosses above the desk to* C)

(MERTON *moves to* L *of the desk*)

(*To Kate*) I wonder—could we find a dressmaker in Venice? Out of one black frock; into another black one. It begins to seem so pointless.

KATE. But they're lovely.

MILLY. No. The badge of the survivor. (*To Merton*) You see, when I was ten years old, there were—with my father and mother —there were five of us. I'm all that's left by now, so black's become a habit. (*She crosses to Susan*) And a habit it would be so nice—it's *time*, to break, I think. (*To Merton*) We'll depend on you, Susie and I, to remember that we're coming.

(SUSAN *and* MILLY *exit down* R, *closing the door behind them.* KATE *moves* RC)

MERTON (*moving down* L *of the desk*) Your message did say seven-thirty?

KATE. When you leave in the afternoon, she usually rests. With Mrs Shepherd hovering. They don't come down till eight. However, here we are—(*with a mock curtsy*) I'm "entertaining" you. (*She moves to the doors up* C *and closes them*) And poor Aunt Maud's beautifying should last at least until—but, just in case her greed for dinner drives her down too early . . . (*She moves to* L *of the wing-chair*)

MERTON (*moving to* R *of the desk*) She won't suspect?

KATE (*shaking her head*) It's working wonderfully—our plan.

MERTON (*sharply*) *Your* plan.

KATE (*crossing above the wing-chair to* L *of the chaise; with a flash of irritation*) Mine, then.

MERTON (*penitently*) Kate . . .

KATE. For how long will your editor let you extend your visit?

MERTON (*puzzled*) I leave next week.

KATE. Impossible.

MERTON. I leave on Saturday.

KATE. Write to him. Tell him—promise him—couldn't they make do with some articles on Venice?

MERTON. Possibly—possibly—I could ask. But why?

KATE. *We* leave next week.

MERTON. "We?"

KATE. My aunt and I. For Greece.

MERTON. Then why in God's name should I stay?

KATE. Aunt Maud wants it.

MERTON. Does she!

KATE. So do I, old boy. It's perfect.

MERTON. I'm to stay alone with Milly?

KATE. Why ever not? You're old enough. (*She sits on the upstage left end of the chaise*) With lots of Mrs Shepherd.

MERTON. Is this *your* plan? Or Mrs Lowder's, when she sent for me.

KATE. Certainly she wouldn't like to leave them here with no-one. But Lady Danby has been offering Lord Mark by every post.

MERTON (*crossing to* L *of Kate*) Your aunt still pins her hopes on him!

KATE. More than ever, now.

MERTON. After last week's snub? He left without even seeing her.

KATE (*smiling*) Awkwardly, not quite. He was here to propose to Milly.

MERTON. What!

KATE. Oh, yes. Clearly. She hasn't tattled, though.

MERTON. Then why?—why follow him?

KATE. He can't very well make up to us here.

MERTON. And you want him to?

KATE. Make up to us? Aunt Maud does, certainly. He's still Lord Mark; still what he was before his try at Milly.

MERTON (*moving down* c *and turning*) So now he's to try at *you?*

KATE. I hope, as in the past, not to let it come to that. But he's nearly penniless. And now he knows he can't have *Milly's* fortune —well, there's only my aunt—only *her* mound of money-bags. So— if he does propose to me, I want you here.

MERTON. Why here?

KATE. You don't think I'll accept him! Aunt Maud is, for the moment, very smug and gratified. Day by day she sees you more and more engrossed by Milly. And when you stay on here alone . . .

MERTON. She won't suspect it's because of me——

KATE. That I decline Lord Mark. And otherwise she would. She'd know. And she has claws. She'd show them.

MERTON. But what's the use . . . ? (*He moves to* L *of the wing-chair*)

KATE. You'd be tabooed. We couldn't even meet.

MERTON (*shrugging*) Well, as things *are* . . . (*He moves up* L *of the wing-chair*)

KATE. This gains us time.

MERTON (*turning to her; with force*) And what's the use of *that?* I'll never ever be the sort of man she wants for you: ruthless, powerful. You must accept me as I am. For time, thank God, won't change me. No more than it will change your aunt.

KATE (*with complete confidence*) It will change everything, my dear. (*She rises*) So write to your editor. (*She moves above the chaise*) I'll go and talk to Milly.

MERTON (*with a step towards her*) Wait a minute.

KATE. It's diplomatic.

MERTON (*moving below the wing-chair*) Do you want her to think you positively hate me?

KATE (*moving to him; severely*) If you spoil this for us now—(*she clasps his hand and smiles*) I truly think I shall.

(SUSAN *enters down* R, *leaving the door open.* KATE *and* MERTON *part quickly.* KATE *moves to the head of the chaise*)

SUSAN (*moving to* R *of the chaise*) Is Maud not down yet?

KATE. No. Why?—are we ready? I was going to Milly.

SUSAN (*sharply*) Don't, my dear. (*She turns, closes the door down* R *then speaks more gently*) Not now.

KATE (*checked by Susan's obvious distraction*) Oh . . . ?

SUSAN (*crossing below the chaise to Merton*) Milly's resting. I'm afraid she must fail us at dinner.

KATE (*moving towards the door down* R) I'll go to her.

SUSAN (*turning quickly*) Later!—please. She might even come down.

MERTON. She isn't ill, then?

SUSAN (*crossing to the doors up* C) No, no, no, no, *no!* She's ever so much better. (*She opens the door*)

(MERTON *moves to the left end of the fireplace*)

(*She turns*) Well, if you'll forgive me, I must just tell Ganaseta . . .

(SUSAN *exits up* C, *closing the door behind her*)

MERTON (*turning to Kate*)  Did she see us?

KATE (*moving to the right end of the fireplace*)  She's too sick with worry to see anything but Milly.

MERTON (*puzzled*)  But she said just now that——

KATE (*cutting in; flatly*)  Milly isn't better; Milly's worse.

MERTON (*after a slight pause*)  Is it her lungs—consumption?

KATE (*shaking her head*)  They can cure that now.

MERTON.  If they take it up in—(*Suddenly*) You mean she can't be cured?

(KATE *does not reply*)

(*He crosses to* LC) When she said just now that her black frocks were the badge of the survivor, I thought, "Yes, that's what you seem: someone saved from the shipwreck." (*He turns to Kate*) But she's come through it—come through her adventure.

KATE (*with a step towards him*)  Her adventure's still to come. Do let her have it.

MERTON.  Her adventure? (*With a puzzled frown*) I only meant she doesn't seem like someone who is dying.

KATE (*sitting* C *of the fender*)  Her pride. Her wonderful, fierce, modest pride. She won't "smell" of drugs; she won't "taste" of medicine. She'll give no more sign than your watch, when you haven't wound it. Nobody but Sir Luke will really know.

MERTON (*sharply*)  Sir Luke? Sir Luke Strett?

(KATE *nods*)

(*He moves to* L *of the wing-chair. Gloomy*) Ahh. Then one seems to guess . . .

KATE.  Don't guess. Do only as I say. (*She rises and moves to the upstage end of the chaise. Sadly and fondly*) She loves life. I want her not to miss the best of it.

MERTON (*with a certain edge*)  That's not all you want.

(KATE *turns, struck by his tone*)

It isn't for her sake I'm to stay. What you're concerned with is to beguile your aunt. (*He moves to* R *of the desk*)

KATE.  True. But I adore Milly. And, if I do use her, I give value in return. (*She moves to* L *of the chaise*) I give—as only you can know— all I have that's precious.

MERTON.  Are you sure I'm yours to give? What have I in return?

KATE (*after a small, surprised pause*)  My love.

MERTON (*coldly*)  Have I, though?

KATE.  You know it. (*With a step towards him*) I've risked every-thing.

MERTON (*moving to* L *of her*)  With your aunt so beguiled, I thought your point was you risk nothing. I want—I need your love. How can I feel it's mine?

KATE.  Can you feel it isn't?

MERTON.  "Giving" me to Milly!

KATE. Oh, let her not miss everything . . . !

MERTON (*bitterly and impatiently*) I know!—and gain us "time". (*He pauses*) Well. *With* you, I can do it. But without you—no. And I must be sure.

(KATE *gives a weary, helpless gesture and moves to the right end of the fireplace*)

If you'll—if you'll come to me . . .

KATE (*turning; in a low voice*) Come to you?

MERTON. If you'll only come to me.

KATE. How? Where?

MERTON (*moving to her*) To my rooms. We can arrange it.

KATE. Is this why you took them?

MERTON. Yes. You knew, I'm sure. (*His hand goes towards her shoulder*)

MAUD (*off up* C) I see, my dear: she'll have a tray. Why don't we all? A picnic!

(KATE *hastily separates from Merton and crosses down* L *of the desk.*
MAUD *enters up* C, *splendidly dressed, leaving the doors open. She carries a feather fan*)

MERTON. Good evening, Mrs Lowder.

MAUD (*greeting them*) Mr Denver—Kate. Oh, Kate—the garnets look splendid! (*She moves to* R *of the desk*) Let me see. Oh, yes—yes. (*With a qualifying frown*) And yet . . . (*An idea*) When worn with pearls, perhaps. A rope of pearls like Milly's.

(KATE *gives a short, humourless laugh*)

But they would suit you so! (*She appeals to Merton*) Wouldn't they?

KATE (*with a rueful smile*) They would. I see myself . . .

MAUD. Buck up! then. Yes—*I* see you—marrying in pearls.

KATE (*equivocally*) You're much too good. (*She turns away to the downstage window*)

MAUD (*snapping*) Am I?—am I? I don't think I am.

KATE. Oh, yes, indeed—you spoil me. (*She sits on the stool down* L)

(MAUD, *after a quick look at Kate, crosses to Merton*)

MAUD. It's not just that she's my niece. I might have had fifty nieces and not cared a tinker's damn for any one of them. In fact, I'd two. The other's nothing; but I marked Kate early on. I appropriated, saved her. Then, like my investments, I let her appreciate.

MERTON. Yes.

KATE (*ironically*) Will it pay, though?

MAUD (*blandly*) With your happiness, my dear, in a great future.

KATE. I mean that to invest is to risk.

MAUD. I take my risks. I understand them. (*To Merton*) I want to see her high—high up—high up and in the light.

MERTON (*moving to the head of the chaise; with dry humour*) Oh, one quite conceives it.

MAUD. But why praise Kate to you? (*She brushes his arm with her feather fan; glibly sentimental*) Don't be too unhappy that Miss Theale fails us at dinner.

MERTON. She isn't really bad, I trust.

MAUD. Oh, dear, no. And for that we've you to thank, dear man. (*She glances at Kate, then back to Merton*) He's been a tonic!—such a tonic!

KATE (*dryly*) Let us patent him, Aunt Maud.

MAUD. But not for general consumption. (*To Merton. With menacing archness*) Only for a very sweet particular person's use. (*She sits in the wing-chair. Business-like*) Susan tells me you've taken rooms. (*Coyly*) I flatter myself I know the reason. (*She waves her fan at Merton*)

(MERTON, *embarrassed, moves and sits on the left side of the chaise*)

(*To Kate*) The duck!—do look—he's quite confused! (*To Merton*) We leave next week to join Lord Mark. (*She shrugs sadly*) It's not my inclination, but Kate wishes it and so! (*Firmly*) You'll stay, however. You've settled.

MERTON. There are all sorts of things to consider.

MAUD. No doubt. There is, above all, the great thing.

MERTON. Which is . . . ?

MAUD. The importance of not losing the occasion of your life. She's charming, she's clever and she's good. (*To Kate*) Isn't she?

KATE. Milly is an angel.

MAUD (*to Merton*) There!—you see?—an angel! With a thumping bank account.

MERTON. I'm much obliged to you for the very handsome offer——

MAUD. Of what doesn't belong to me? It could belong to *you*. So stay.

MERTON. Miss Croy has been persuading me.

MAUD (*with a look at Kate*) She but preaches what she practises; she'll do anything for her friend.

MERTON. I don't resist, you know. I find Miss Theale charming.

MAUD (*suddenly and for the first time genuinely warm to him*) Of course —of course. I know. I've seen.

(SUSAN *enters up* C *and moves above the desk.* KATE *rises*)

SUSAN. They're ready for us. You'll understand—I haven't dressed.

(MERTON *rises*)

MAUD. (*rising and moving to* L *of the wing-chair*) In your wonderful country, does one dress? I've often meant to ask. Mr Denver, you'll bring my niece in, since Milly—(*To Susan*) Must she fail us?

SUSAN. I'm afraid so.

MAUD Oh, dear. (*moving to the doors up* C; *cosily to Susan*) Now then, what was I saying? (*Remembering*) Oh, why, yes—of course. (*She goes into the hall. Over her shoulder*) In your wonderful country, does one dress?

C

(MAUD *exits up* C)

SUSAN (*moving to the doors up* C) Well, Maud, in Boston—certainly.

(SUSAN *exits up* C)

MERTON (*moving to* R *of the wing-chair*) I will stay. If you'll come to me.

KATE (*moving to the doors up* C) Quickly——

MERTON. But if not, I'll do nothing. I'll leave before you.

(KATE *turns anxiously to him*)

I'll leave tomorrow.

KATE. Quickly——

MERTON. Will you?

KATE (*after a slight pause*) Yes.

KATE *and* MERTON *exit up* C *as—*

*the* CURTAIN *falls*

# ACT II

## SCENE I

SCENE—*The same. Five days later. Morning.*

*When the* CURTAIN *rises, the doors up* C *are open.* MAUD *is seated at the desk. Four small envelopes, containing tips, lie on the blotter in front of her.* SUSAN *is standing* L *of Maud.*

MAUD (*picking up the envelopes and checking through them*) Aldo, Italo, Maria, Ganaseta. (*She puts down the envelopes and prepares to write on another*) And what's the cook's name?

SUSAN. "Assunta."

(MAUD *writes*)

(*She peers over Maud's shoulder*) No, two s's, dear.

MAUD (*peevishly making the correction*) What Assunta-with-two-s's really deserves—(*she puts six lira notes in the envelope*) is a few sharp words on the use of garlic. (*She puts the envelope with the others*) However . . . ! There. That does it.

SUSAN. And Pasquale?

MAUD. Pasquale! Not a penny! Or, this morning, at last, has he deigned to take us?

(KATE *enters down* R, *dressed ready to depart. She closes the door and moves to* R *of the chaise*)

SUSAN. If there's too much luggage, I suppose, for Italo alone.

MAUD (*to Kate*) They haven't brought the bags down?

KATE. No, not yet. There's time.

MAUD. I've done our tips for the staff. (*She rises and picks up the envelopes*) So shall we go and puncture their—no doubt—inflated hopes?

KATE. Oh, I did mine last night.

MAUD. You what? (*She moves to* L *of the chaise and confronts Kate*)

(MERTON *enters up* C)

MERTON (*moving to* R *of the arch*) Good morning.

(KATE *nods a cool acknowledgement*)

SUSAN. Good morning, Mr Denver.

MAUD (*glaring at Kate and brandishing the envelopes*) These were to be from both of us! (*She crosses to the desk. To Merton; briefly*) Good morning.

MERTON. Good morning.

MAUD (*hardly waiting for him to finish*) Very well, then!—I'll have to take some out. (*She sits at the desk and extracts some notes from the envelopes*) Over-tipping just encourages unsuitable ideas. (*She turns suddenly to Kate*) What about Pasquale?

KATE. Yes.

MAUD (*very cross*) You tipped Pasquale? Why?

KATE (*wandering slowly around the chaise to L of it; smiling*) For the very reason that makes you so indignant.

MAUD. What?—pray?

KATE. Oh, for his beauty, Aunt——

MAUD. I beg your——!

(KATE *coolly raises her hand to check Maud's indignation*)

KATE. —in waiting with such patience for dear Milly's need of him. (*She sits on the left side of the chaise*)

MAUD (*taking a fresh envelope*) "Patience"—hmpph! Laziness. (*She writes on the envelope*) But, since *you*'ve tipped him, I must. One can imagine only too vividly what use he'll put it to. (*She transfers some bank-notes*) A little of Assunta's-with-two-s's, then. A very, very little. And, Mr Denver, I'll depend on you to see Pasquale earns it.

MERTON (*with a step* C) Willingly. But how?

MAUD. Susan says that she and Milly are to visit you for tea. (*She rises and moves to Merton*) Let there be many other such delectable excursions.

SUSAN (*moving* LC) Please don't think me pressing, but you know, until that evening, she had no wish to go—well, really anywhere.

MAUD. Parish feasts, autumn sunsets, Veronese, Titian—would she budge? But tea with Mr Denver . . . ! (*She moves to the doors up* C *and turns to Susan*) Oh!—we leave you in good hands.

(MAUD *exits up* C, *taking the envelopes with her*)

SUSAN (*to Merton*) I'll tell Milly that you're here. (*She moves to the doors up* C *and turns*) And again—please—you won't think I was pressing?

MERTON. Of course not, Mrs Shepherd.

SUSAN. Thank you. You're so kind.

(SUSAN *exits up* C. MERTON *crosses quickly to the doors up* C, *closes them, then moves to* L *of Kate*)

MERTON. All the same, you know—Milly will not come for tea.

KATE (*rising*) Oh, yes. For a while, at least, I'm sure that she'll be able.

MERTON (*holding her by the waist*) To the Piazza, then—to Florian's. But to my rooms—(*He shakes his head*) Not Milly Theale; not Susan Shepherd; no-one. Only you. Alone there with me. Still. (*He bends to kiss her*)

(KATE *turns away and faces down* R)

KATE. Please. I'll cry. I mustn't.

(MERTON *moves behind Kate, holds her arms and speaks over her left shoulder*)

MERTON. And when I leave here every evening, I'll know that you are waiting. I'll turn the key, push the door, step in, and you'll be there.

KATE. I love you. You are free. But I'm engaged to you for ever.

MERTON. And I to you.

KATE (*half turning to him*) No. You are free. Remember that.

MERTON. Free . . . (*Sharply*) Why?

KATE (*crossing below the desk*) Because it's true.

MERTON (*firmly*) Never, now. It can't be.

KATE (*moving to the downstage window*) And we've told too many lies.

MERTON. I, my dear, have told none.

KATE (*turning to look at him*) And I've told none—to you.

MERTON (*moving below the wing-chair; cold and strong*) Then answer: why must I be free?

KATE (*moving up L of the desk; with a sudden smile*) Tush, tush, tush —buck up, old boy! (*She moves above the desk*) I shan't sacrifice you! Haven't I just sworn that I'm engaged to you for ever? And I would wait for ever. But—as things are—there'll be no need. Buck up! There'll be no sacrifice. Of you, or me—(*with a change of tone*) or Milly.

(MERTON *moves to R of Kate and stares at her. After a pause he speaks without inflexion*)

MERTON. Kate, what more do you want now?

KATE. What more? I want, I'm trying—(*she looks away from him*) and shall try—for everything, my dear.

MERTON. Be explicit.

KATE (*moving to the downstage window; with her back to him*) No. Oh, no . . . !

MERTON (*after a pause*) Have I begun to bore you?

(KATE *turns to him, puzzled*)

(*He moves to R of the desk*) I remember, months and months ago, one night at Mrs Lowder's: a dinner-party—but you weren't my neighbour; you were seated across and several places down from me. When I discreetly could, I watched you—talking, laughing. (*He shrugs*) With whom—I've quite forgotten. I remember only you. And my sudden wave of panic: "What if, in time, I should begin to bore this creature!" (*He moves to R of the desk chair.*) How cunning Mrs Lowder was to have invited me! All your talent for life—your direct, your splendid talent—was on show there, was the showpiece, and it was splendid, Kate. But my talent for life— well, at Mrs Lowder's table, what a poor, little, weak thing I knew *that* must seem! Patched up for the occasion; like my dinner jacket. But I'm not talking now about my wretched want of means. (*He moves up* L *of the desk*) I'm talking about the different ways we've been made as people, the different ways in which we approach life. I admired your way—but, even more, I was frightened by it, Kate.

KATE (*with an uneasy gaiety*) Oh?—however, you've survived!

MERTON (*with an ironic smile*) Well, I wonder. Have I? (*He nods and moves* C) With some effort. (*Coldly*) At some cost.

KATE. And for some reward, surely. At what others—though not I—might look on as *my* cost.

(MERTON *turns to her*)

My coming to you.

MERTON (*moving below the desk*) Oh, Kate, I didn't mean—! Forgive me.

KATE (*smiling fondly and shaking her head*) If you desert me over this—never, never, never.

MERTON (*his rush of emotion checked*) Over what, Kate?

(KATE *is impassive*)

*Over what?*

KATE. Your being free, of course. (*She crosses below Merton to* C) And I shan't be more explicit, so don't ask me again. I shan't do *all* the work for you. If you want things named—(*she turns to him*) name them.

MERTON (*slowly turning to face her*) Since Miss Theale is to die, I'm to marry her . . . ?

(KATE *holds his eyes but does not reply*)

So that after her death, I shall have her money . . . ?

KATE (*holding his eyes*) Yes.

(*There is a pause during which neither moves*)

(*She looks away*) Yes—yes. (*She glances quickly at Merton, then moves to the fireplace, and turns. With complete control and almost lightly*) Or do you wash your hands of me?

MERTON (*almost pleasantly*) And that's why I'm to stay on here; that's why I am "free". (*He sighs*) I knew your aunt wanted this . . .

KATE. She thinks it will make Milly live.

MERTON (*moving up* C) But never, never, Kate, that *you* . . . (*He turns on her with a harder note*) And if Miss Theale does not accept me?

KATE. You can but try, my dear.

MERTON. "Try." With a dying girl!

KATE (*with force*) For you, she isn't dying! (*She moves towards him. Patiently*) And to stay is to try. At least, it will appear so.

MERTON (*startled*) Appear so to Milly?

KATE (*smiling*) Why, of course.

MERTON (*a sudden, trapped sensation*) What shall I say, then? What's my reason—my excuse for staying on?

(KATE *smiles and shakes her head*)

How can I face her? I must have an excuse.

KATE (*fondly indulgent*) If you like. But there's no need.

MERTON (*looking away from her*) It's your idea that she may *offer* marriage?

KATE (*with a non-committal shrug*) In the manner of princesses.

MERTON. It will have to come that way.

KATE. And you'll accept.

MERTON. But can you *like* it?

KATE. I'm a person, thank Heaven, who can do what I don't like.

MERTON (*taking her by the hand*) If it's for you, then, so can I.

KATE. Good; good. (*She crosses towards the door down* R) Do you still think that we approach life so very differently? (*She turns, moves to* L *of the chaise and holds out a hand*) Come, say good-bye now to Aunt Maud.

MERTON (*moving to her*) First to you. (*He takes her hand and tries to pull her back*)

KATE (*turning from him; tears suddenly behind her voice*) We've said it.

MERTON. You will write.

KATE. Letters? Think of it. Impossible.

MERTON. See here, you know—in Greece . . .

KATE (*turning to him*) Yes . . .?

MERTON. Don't—don't . . .

KATE. Don't what?

MERTON. Don't fail me. It would kill me, Kate.

MILLY (*off up* C; *calling*) Kate . . . ?

KATE (*calling*) I'm here . . . !

(MERTON *crosses to the left end of the fireplace.* KATE *moves down* L *of the chaise.*

MILLY *enters up* C, *leaving the doors open*)

MILLY (*to Kate*) Have you got the keys? Your aunt wants her cases locked before Pasquale takes them.

KATE (*to herself*) Have I . . . ?

MILLY. Pasquale is pretending to be terribly offended.

KATE (*smiling*) Oh, dear! (*Remembering*) Yes, of course—they're in my bag.

MERTON (*moving to the doors up* C) I'll tell Mrs Lowder, shall I? I'm going, anyway, to bid her *bon voyage*.

MILLY. Good morning, Mr Denver.

MERTON. Good morning.

MILLY (*cheerfully*) Except it's such a sad one, really, isn't it?

KATE (*to Merton*) My bag's on the small escritoire.

MERTON. I'll tell her.

KATE. Thank you.

MILLY. And for Pasquale's sake, if you could add—oh, well, something like: how much more honest than the English all Italians are.

(MERTON *smiles and exits up* C)

(*She calls after him*) Tactfully, but loud enough for him to overhear! (*She closes the doors, turns to Kate, beaming, then goes to her, holding out her hands*)

(KATE *lightly grasps Milly's hands*)

Don't leave me, Kate. Must you? Yes, I suppose you must. Oh, well!

KATE (*smiling*) You needn't look so happy.

MILLY. Kate! I don't—I'm not!

KATE. *I'm* not, certainly. Back into harness, though!

MILLY (*crossing below Kate to R of her*) It's strange . . .

KATE. What . . . ?

MILLY (*sitting on the end of the chaise, facing L*) Isn't it strange . . . ? that Mr Denver should be staying . . .

KATE (*moving to L of Milly*) Don't try to see around too many corners, Milly; not, that is, when a little peep around just one will serve. That Mr Denver should be staying seems to me quite simple, just as it seems quite simple that you should want him to. You're both—I mean this kindly; in your case, lovingly—you're both quite simple people. Be simple; let him be. Leave Aunt Maud, Lord Mark, Kate Croy to be what you call "strange". Strange in their diplomacy. Strange to *you*, I mean, because, of course, they—*we* know each other well.

MILLY (*wondering*) You sound as if—(*She puts away the thought with a smile and a shake of her head*) That's silly!

KATE. Tell me.

MILLY. As if you don't much like them.

KATE. Or myself. I don't.

MILLY. Kate . . . !

KATE. Unhappily, I see things as they are; I always have. And that's why I'm sad to leave you.

MILLY. But you want to be with him . . . ?

KATE. Lord Mark? (*With an ironic smile*) Well, since Aunt Maud does.

MILLY. He's a very great person. And so, of course, is she.

KATE (*with delighted incredulity*) My aunt? She isn't anyone, poor woman; she isn't anything. (*She gives a short, humourless laugh and crosses to the downstage window*) Of course, she isn't "poor", either. And with Lord Mark, oh!—that's what weighs.

MILLY. How horrid, Kate.

KATE (*turning*) Not them; they've quite a happy understanding. He weighs her purse; she weighs his name—the London salons, country houses—to all of which Lord Mark's name is an open sesame. (*She moves up L of the desk*) Can the system be so very different in Boston or New York?

MILLY (*at sea*) I don't know.

KATE. But while you were in London—you must at least have sensed how society works there. Anybody who has anything to offer—position, money, beauty, power—works it where he can.

MILLY. "Works it?"

KATE. Bargains—(*she moves up* R *of the desk*) on the social market. Tries to get a more than equal value in return. And people can quite like each other in the midst of it. As my aunt quite likes Lord Mark, and as he quite likes her. Unless he's even more of a hypocrite than she thinks.

MILLY. You mean, she doesn't trust him . . . ?

KATE. No . . . !

MILLY. Because they're bargaining?

KATE (*moving down* R *of the desk*) Waiting, both of them, for what the other will put down.

MILLY. And Mrs Lowder puts down you?

KATE. I'm part of what she offers.

MILLY. But, since she doesn't trust him, keeps a firm grip?

KATE. Lest he should grab and run? (*She smiles*) No, Lord Mark's not ready.

MILLY. Oh . . . ?

KATE. At one time, he was. (*She moves below the wing-chair*) And I was on the counter. But then a certain young American appeared. Poor Aunt Maud! She had to whisk her goods back into the shop-window.

MILLY (*troubled to express it without hurting Kate*) Kate. Lord Mark knows now that I—well, that I can never be an alternative.

KATE (*moving to* L *of Milly; gaily*) Does he? Truly, truly?

MILLY. Shall I swear it?

KATE. No!

MILLY (*taking Kate's hand*) But there it is. "Truly, truly." Please don't mind him asking me. Please don't think less of him. (*She releases Kate's hand. Lamely and awkwardly*) Because, after all, an ambitious man must have lots of ideas.

KATE (*moving above the wing-chair*) Oh, the more the merrier! If I end up as the best of them.

MILLY. You will. Give him time.

KATE. To give is Aunt Maud's province.

MILLY. Her wonderful generosity . . . !

KATE. "Her wonderful—" (*Dryly*) Well.

MILLY. You said just now, for instance, she's been put out by me. And yet she's still so beautifully kind.

KATE (*laughing*) Ninny! (*She leans over the back of the wing-chair*) You put her in much more than you ever put her out. You arrived in London like manna from Heaven delivered to her door. You're not, like us, you see, "placed" on the London social scale: hideously further down than lots and lots of others. You could do anything; everyone wanted you; we clutched your petticoat. We've been of no real use to you. You're of use to us, but that's a different matter. Of use to us in so many ways, Milly! Some, you can scarce suspect. Oh, a fiendishly bad bargain, dear!—you could have done so much better. If I were to give you my honest advice, I'd say, "Drop us while you can." We don't want you to, of course, so it's decent of me to tell you. But—(*she moves to* L *of Milly*) Mrs Shepherd's school-day follies—well, why should you have to pay so dreadfully for them?

MILLY (*fascinated, horrified and bewildered, but trying to be amused*) Kate!—for Susan's schooldays . . . ?

KATE.   When she first met that natural, forceful handful—my Aunt Maud.

MILLY.   Without that—without Susie, I should never have met *you*.

KATE.   Oh, you may very well loathe me yet!

MILLY (*rising*) Kate! Why say such things?

KATE (*wincing*) Because you're a dove. (*She kisses Milly lightly, almost formally*)

MILLY (*with a sigh of relief*) Ohh—is *that* what's wrong? (*She resumes her seat*) Too soft, too weak, you mean? (*Prosaically*) But then, a dove has wide, strong wings.

KATE (*a lightly ironic warning*) To fly. To fly with.

MILLY (*after a moment of grave consideration*) Or protect.

(SUSAN *enters up* C. *She wears her hat and coat and is carrying her own and Kate's handbags. She moves down* L *of the wing-chair, leaving the doors open*)

SUSAN (*to Kate*) Everything else is in the gondolas. I've brought your bag.

(KATE *moves to Susan, takes her bag, then goes to the left end of the fireplace*)

KATE.   Oh—we're leaving, then. It suddenly seems real.

SUSAN (*to Milly*) I thought, if you don't mind, I'd go along and wave.

MILLY.   Yes, Susie, do.

SUSAN (*moving up* L *of the desk*) I'll be back in time for luncheon with you and Mr Denver.

(MAUD *enters up* C *and goes to Kate.*
MERTON *follows her on*)

MAUD (*indignantly*) Just how many lira did you distribute, Kate? My tips were received—(*to Milly*) oh, politely—(*to Kate*) but in a more than somewhat anticlimactic atmosphere. (*She moves to* L *of Milly*) Well! You hospitable thing, you dear, dear child—no, we won't say good-bye, but rather, *au revoir*.

MILLY.   *Au revoir*, dear Mrs Lowder.

MAUD.   Yes—*au revoir*. Because after this—the wonderful country of your birth must simply do without you. Return to *us*. That's understood. Stay among us; you must stay. Anything else is impossible and ridiculous. (*She takes Milly's hands*) You must make your home with us. (*She releases Milly's hands and moves to the doors up* C) Mustn't she, Kate?—mustn't she, Susan? (*Even more richly glib*) Mustn't she, dear Mr Denver? (*She turns to Milly*) Be an obedient thing, now!—return to us! *Arividerci!*

(Maud *blows Milly a farewell kiss and exits up* c)

Susan (*following Maud*)  Maud, you're to ride with Pasquale. I've arranged to have the luggage put in Italo's gondola.

(Susan *exits up* c. Kate *smiles at Milly, moves to her and kisses her*)

Kate.  Milly . . .

Milly.  Kate . . .

Kate.  Good-bye.

(Kate, *smiling tenderly, gazes at Milly for a long moment, then abruptly turns and goes quickly to the doors up* c. *As she passes* Merton, *she pauses almost imperceptibly and nods a farewell, without meeting his eyes*)

Mr Denver.

Merton.  Good-bye, Miss Croy.

(Kate, *without looking back, exits up* c. Merton *closes the doors after her*)

Milly (*moving to the fireplace*)  You won't go down . . . ?

Merton.  Will you . . . ?

Milly.  No—it's all been said.

Merton (*moving* c)  *I* feel that, rather.

(Milly *is shy and a little awkward in approaching the question she wants to ask*)

Milly.  Oh, dear!—think of all the other good-byes if you'd been going, too.

(Merton *smiles and, dreading the question which he knows is approaching, moves down* c)

I mean, going back to London.

Merton.  Yes.

Milly (*moving to the head of the chaise; embarrassed*)  It's so nice that you're not. For a while, anyway. (*She turns to him, in a fluster*) Oh!— I didn't mean nice just for a *while*!

Merton (*turning to her; not understanding*)  I'm sorry, I . . . ?

Milly.  I said—(*She moves to* l *of the chaise*) No, let it go!—I didn't mean it. What I *did* mean is we're glad that you can stay.

Merton.  Thank you. I am, too.

Milly.  Oh, good! (*She pauses and wanders below the chaise to* r *of it*) We thought you might be under orders—bothersome, officious ones.

Merton (*startled*)  Orders? Why? Whose?

Milly.  Your manager—your editor—is that what he'd be called? (*She moves to the head of the chaise*) I seem to have read or been told or something, that newspapermen must always wait till Fleet Street gives them orders. Wait wherever they find themselves.

Merton (*relieved and smiling*)  But not on holiday!

Milly (*grasping the word and moving to him*)  Holiday. Ah, yes. Then you're still here for that.

Merton.  Oh, well!—(*he moves to* r *of the desk chair; embarrassed*) for me, between work and play—there's not much difference.

MILLY (*happy to be on firm ground*) I see. You'll do some work here too.

MERTON (*still floundering, but concealing the fact*) A little quiet writing. So impossible in London! For a long time now, I've hoped, I've planned . . . (*He hesitates*)

MILLY. Yes . . . ?

MERTON. Not planned, perhaps, so much as dreamed . . . (*Suddenly the lie is produced almost explosively*) I've an idea for a book.

MILLY (*moving quickly below the wing-chair; enraptured*) A book . . . ! Ohh—! (*With excitement*) You'll do it here?

MERTON. I—I hope to begin.

MILLY. You haven't yet?

MERTON (*moving to L of the desk*) Well, only just.

MILLY. And since you came?

MERTON. A few days ago I thought that I had broken ground. (*Hoping to leave the subject*) But don't let's go into that.

MILLY (*cutting in; with concern*) You should have said! (*She sits in the wing-chair*) We've made a terrible mess of your time.

MERTON (*moving below the desk; smiling*) Of course you have. Now I'm hanging on to tidy up.

MILLY (*enthusiastically*) You'll want the best part of your days.

MERTON. Oh, I shall make do with the worst.

MILLY. No, please.

MERTON (*moving to her*) The best must be for you.

MILLY. Your rooms are quiet? You can work there?

MERTON (*apprehensively*) My rooms? Oh, yes. Yes—perfectly. (*He crosses below Milly to the head of the chaise*)

MILLY (*after a brief pause*) You will remember, won't you, that Susie and I are coming . . . ?

MERTON (*casting about for a way to avoid committal*) Of course—of course. (*He turns to her*) But you—your custom of not going out: will it be safe to break it?

MILLY (*sharply*) "Safe"?

(*There is a pause in which* MERTON *inwardly winces for his mistake*)

You suppose me so very bad?

MERTON. One sees—one can't help seeing—that you do take certain precautions.

MILLY (*denying this interpretation*) No!

MERTON. I'll believe whatever you tell me.

MILLY. Good. Well, then, I'm splendid.

MERTON (*smiling*) Oh, I don't need you to tell me that.

MILLY. I mean, that I want so to live—! (*She pauses with the intensity of it*)

MERTON (*prompting her*) Yes?

MILLY. Well, that I know I *can*.

MERTON (*her intensity unnerves him and he retreats into playfulness*) Whatever you do?

MILLY. Whatever I do. If I want to live, I can.

MERTON (*sitting on the left side of the chaise; suddenly pained with pity*) Ah, then—that I believe.

MILLY. I will, I will.

MERTON (*very moved*) You must.

MILLY (*prosaically; almost mulish*) Well, then, if you say that, why mayn't we come for tea?

MERTON (*lightly*) Will it help you?

MILLY (*gaily*) Every little helps! And it's very little indeed for me to stay at home. (*After a short pause. Wistfully*) Only, I shan't want to miss it——

MERTON (*prompting her*) Yes?

MILLY. On the day you *do* say "come".

MERTON (*warmly and clearly*) You may come whenever you like.

MILLY. Oh—I'm being a terrible bore! (*She springs up and moves to* R *of the desk*)

(MERTON *rises*)

And sooner than have a silly upset, you might go. So it's no matter.

MERTON (*genuinely protesting*) No matter?

MILLY (*lightly*) We want you not to.

MERTON (*shaking his head*) I won't go.

MILLY (*cheerfully*) Then *I* won't! It's a bargain.

MERTON. You mean—won't come for tea?

MILLY. No—never, now. It's over. And, truly, it's all right. (*She pauses and moves to* R *of the desk chair*) But you do believe me?— I shouldn't have dreamed of venturing out if it *had* been unwise. Because of my health. Or anything. (*She has been intensely shy about this reassurance and ends with a lame little laugh*) Oh, you'd have to force me!

MERTON (*smiling encouragement*) Force you?—you, of all people!

MILLY. Because I'm—so free . . . ?

MERTON. More than anyone else in the world.

MILLY (*qualifying*) Well . . . (*She moves to* L *of the wing-chair. Happily*) And now—about your book.

MERTON (*having forgotten it*) My book—?

MILLY. The one that nothing will induce me to run the risk of spoiling.

MERTON (*after a slight pause; firmly*) I'm not doing a book.

MILLY (*mystified*) Not?—you're not writing?

MERTON (*moving above the chaise; with great relief at abandoning the lie*) I don't know what I'm doing.

MILLY (*gravely and tentatively*) Then, if it's not for your book . . . ?

MERTON (*turning to her*) What *am* I staying for?

MILLY. I mean, with all your London work, with all you have to do. Isn't it rather empty for you?

MERTON. Empty? (*Vaguely*) Oh, well . . . ! (*He moves to* R *of the chaise*)

MILLY (*moving up* L *of the desk*) I ask too many questions. (*She lightly settles the matter*) You stay because you've got to.

MERTON (*rejecting the suggestion and looking at her*) No. Isn't it enough to stay, after all, for *you?*

MILLY (*in a small voice*) For me . . . Oh, you must judge.

MERTON. Well, then, so long as I remain, please take it that I do.

MILLY (*smiling*) Thank you, Mr Denver.

MERTON (*frowning*) No, please don't! Don't *thank* me.

MILLY. Why? Is it in some way clumsy? Yes—your face says so. (*She crosses to Merton, to put him at his ease, turns on the spontaneous, slightly comical American girl*) Oh, dear!—what a problem to be American! After all these months away from home, still one hasn't got the rules. What to say, when to say it—and, of course, most important of all: what not even to whisper! (*She crosses towards the door down R and suggests parenthetically*) Shall we do our usual stroll through my hired palazzo?

(MERTON *moves quickly to the door down R and opens it*)

Sometimes, when I've looked back on London conversations, I've wondered, "What in the world *did* they say?—while making such a perfect success out of what was never mentioned!"

(MERTON *laughs*)

(*She crosses below Merton to the door down R and exits.* MERTON *follows her off and her voice fades away*) (*Off*) Now, in America, you know, there are certain things one doesn't dare discuss. But in England—whatever the topic—somehow, all those perfect manners smooth you safely through . . .

*the* CURTAIN *falls*

SCENE 2

SCENE—*The same. Three weeks later. Afternoon.*

*When the* CURTAIN *rises,* MILLY *is seated in the wing-chair, entertaining Merton to tea.* MERTON *is seated on a small stool, R of Milly. A small tea-table, with a tray and silver tea-service is between them and a tiered cake-stand is L of Milly. They have practically finished their meal and now talk in the cosy half-light formed by the glowing fire and the setting sun.* MILLY's *speech begins before the* CURTAIN *rises.*

MILLY. "Poor dears," I thought, when their letter came, "to them I'm a terrible orphaned duty—I really must let them off with some polite excuse". Wasn't it lucky that I couldn't think of one? Because, of course, it was in Boston that I met Susan Shepherd. Right away we hit it off—oh, tremendously! I'd never met anyone like her; her interests, her knowledge—of books, you know, and things. And when I was back in New York again, I missed her dreadfully. So I sent her a wire: "Come to Europe, Susie." And straight away we *did*! (*She looks towards the downstage window*) Isn't it getting dark early? Compared with—just three weeks ago, say, when the others left for Greece.

MERTON. Mmm. Looks to me as if the weather's due to change.

MILLY. Do you think a lamp . . . ?

MERTON (*rising and crossing to the desk*) Good idea. (*He picks up a box of matches from the desk and lights the lamp on the right end of the desk*)

MILLY. It might be cosier. (*She happily takes in the room*) Tea by lamplight! It *must* be winter. What heaven to be here! There'll be frost on the windows in New York now, and outside—piles of snow. Carriages stuck in it; coachmen cursing; horses whinnying. On wintry days, the horses grow little twin icicles. (*She illustrates with tea-spoons held up under her nose*) See? Like a walrus's whiskers. The longer you drive, the longer they grow. Then, back in the nice, warm, smelly stables—drip, drip, drip away.

MERTON. Don't you miss it at all? (*He picks up the lamp and moves to the table* R *of the arch*)

MILLY (*gravely shaking her head*) I don't know why—or what it is that I've found here.

(MERTON *looks at Milly, places the lamp on the table* R *of the arch then resumes his seat on the stool*)

In London, people used to ask, "*Why* have you come to Europe?" One couldn't say, "I was sad; I was lonely." Even *I* knew *that* would stop conversation dead! I thought of answering, "To see all the things I've read about," but never did—for fear that then they might find out just how little I had read! So, finally, I'd murmur, "Oh—pictures and so on and so forth," because that's what's expected from an American. Expected, but never believed.

MERTON (*smiling*) I believe it. (*He drinks his tea*)

MILLY (*laughing with astonishment*) Why?

MERTON. Well—(*he puts down his cup*) I met you first, if you'll remember, at the National Gallery with Miss Croy.

MILLY. Ah, no! I was quite alone. Kate was with—(*She breaks off, confused*)

MERTON (*calmly*) Miss Croy was with me. Yes.

MILLY. I mean that, had *I* been with Kate—well, she'd have brought me for the pictures, wouldn't she?

MERTON. *Weren't* you there for the pictures?

MILLY (*a little shamefaced*) I used to like watching the lady-copyists.

MERTON. The lady-copyists . . . ?

MILLY. Yes. (*On the defensive*) I used to like to watch them work-ing. At their easels with—you know—brushes, tubes of colour . . .

MERTON (*smiling fondly*) In their spectacles and aprons . . .

MILLY (*still on the defensive*) Yes! Is that so strange?

MERTON. When I was a boy, we lived on the Continent in—oh, I suppose a dozen or more English settlements: Lisbon, Rome, and so on. My father was a chaplain; he'd be billeted here and there. And my mother copied famous pictures in the great museums.

MILLY (*thrilled and moved*) No . . . !

MERTON. Then, as now, museums swarmed with copyists, of course. But my mother was better than most. Her work invariably sold.

MILLY (*sighing*) Oh, how I wish I'd known her . . . !

(SUSAN *enters up* C, *leaving the doors open.* MERTON *rises to* R *of his stool*)

SUSAN (*moving up* R *of the desk chair*) Milly, dear—excuse me; excuse me, Mr Denver—but Signora Fagioli has arrived.

MILLY (*remembering*) Of course! (*She rises and moves to* R *of Susan*)

SUSAN. Ganaseta's taken her to your room; so if you've finished tea . . . ?

MILLY (*to Merton*) Signora Fagioli is a seamstress.

MERTON. Oh. Anyway, it's time for me to be off. (*He makes a movement to go*)

MILLY (*urgently*) Not yet—please! I want more about your mother. (*She moves towards the doors up* C) The signora won't mind—come up with me—do!

SUSAN. Mildred Theale!

MILLY (*turning*) But, Susie, there's a screen in there—I'll undress behind it.

SUSAN (*with a little mock gasp of feigned shock*) Off with you! (*She bustles Milly to the door*)

MILLY (*accepting defeat*) Oh, well . . . (*To Merton*) Until eight, then?

MERTON. Eight o'clock.

MILLY. And if the frock's finished—(*she strikes a comic pose, half in and half out of the doors*) prepare to be dumbfounded!

(MILLY *exits up* C. MERTON *moves above the chaise.* SUSAN *closes the doors and moves* C)

SUSAN. I'm so glad you're here.

MERTON. It's a very wonderful experience. (*He gives a startled laugh*) Good heavens!—that was pure American!

SUSAN. Was it? (*She moves to* L *of the wing-chair*) Certainly, it's all I've hoped you might be feeling.

MERTON (*uneasy and covering up with playfulness*) American?

(SUSAN *turns his joke aside with a perfunctory smile*)

SUSAN. If I weren't afraid, there are things I'd like to say.

MERTON. And what are you afraid of, please?

SUSAN. Oh—spoiling other things. Besides, I don't have the chance. You are always with her.

MERTON. I'm not with her now.

SUSAN (*crossing to the fire and warming her hands*) I do so hope that you'll stay on, that you'll be faithful to us.

MERTON. I wonder—will you understand? There are necessities . . .

SUSAN. The daily task and the daily wage? *I* understand, of course. Aren't they just what, in a sense, *I* have given up? She's my princess, you see.

MERTON (*gently*) Not mine, though.

SUSAN. Can't she ever be?

(GANASETA *enters up* C, *carrying a lighted lamp*)

GANASETA. *Permesso, signora?*

SUSAN (*turning, startled*) Yes?—yes? What is it, Ganaseta?

GANASETA. *La lampada, signora.*

SUSAN. Very well, then. Very well.

(MARIA, *the housemaid, enters up* C, *carrying two lighted lamps.* GANASETA *places his lamp on the table between the windows.* MARIA *places one lamp on the table* R *of the doors up* C. GANASETA *takes the other lamp from Maria, indicates the cake-stand, then puts the lamp on the right end of the mantelpiece*)

(*To Merton, apologizing for the intrusion*) I'm sorry . . . But when one lives at court . . . ! The court of a princess . . .

(MARIA *picks up the cake-stand*)

Oh, thank you, Maria.

(MARIA *exits up* C *with the cake-stand.*
    GANASETA *picks up the tea-table and follows Maria off*)

(*To Merton*) Of the heir to all the ages . . . ! (*She indicates the lamp between the windows*) You don't think that lamp is smoking? I'm not sure that I know how to ask him in Italian.

MERTON (*crossing to the lamp* L) Let me do it. (*He adjusts the lamp*)

SUSAN. Thank you.

(GANASETA *enters up* C *and goes to the upstage window*)

No, Ganaseta, leave the curtains.

GANASETA. Signora?

SUSAN (*nervously motioning him out*) Leave the curtains. We may want to watch the sun set.

GANASETA (*blankly acquiescent*) *Prego, signora.*

(GANASETA *exits up* C, *closing the door behind him*)

SUSAN. Of course, she's not your princess. You must do something first. (*She moves to the wing-chair*)

(MERTON *considers his reply as he finishes with the lamp*)

MERTON. Have I done nothing, Mrs Shepherd?

SUSAN. Oh, you've been wonderful!

D

MERTON (*moving to* L *of the desk; slowly and with careful emphasis*) I feel I can't do more.

SUSAN (*bravely, but in despair*) Oh . . . no . . . ?

MERTON. Not so much "can't" as "mustn't".

SUSAN (*in a whisper*) Why?

MERTON (*crossing above the desk to Susan*) Dear Mrs Shepherd, because of the truth. The truth about Milly. The truth that's fenced off here with an expensive vagueness—with smiles and silences and fictions, all strained to breaking-point.

SUSAN. I don't understand . . .

MERTON. No, nobody consents to. (*He crosses above Susan to the right end of the mantelpiece and with his back to Susan, adjusts the lamp*) We all pretend that Milly's portrait of herself is quite, quite perfect, and that nobody has noticed it's hanging by a thread. But one false step . . .

SUSAN (*not looking at him; bravely completing his unspoken thought*) Might—as they say—snap the thread. Is that what you mean?

MERTON. And send her proud, brave portrait crashing. One false step from me.

SUSAN (*turning to him*) And so you walk on tip-toe?

MERTON. Walk on tip-toe. (*He turns to her*) Yes.

(*There is a pause as* SUSAN *sits in the wing-chair*)

SUSAN. I may be wrong. I may be wrong—(*hopefully*) but I've believed her so much better.

MERTON (*moving to* L *of the chaise; kindly*) Isn't that the first of all our fictions, though?

(*Not understanding his point,* SUSAN's *look questions him*)

Always, always, since I came, Milly has been "better".

SUSAN (*thinking that he is confirming her hope*) Since you came. Since you stayed. And so don't say you can't do more.

(MILLY *enters down* R)

You can do everything.

MILLY (*cheerfully*) What can Mr Denver do? (*She closes the door and moves to the head of the chaise*)

SUSAN. Milly, dear! (*She rises and crosses to the lamp* L) I—I—these lamps are so unlike our nice reliable Boston ones! But Mr Denver managed.

MERTON (*moving to the door up* C) And he really must go now. (*He opens the doors*)

MILLY (*crossing to* C; *to Merton*) My frock will be ready!

MERTON (*smiling*) Good.

(MERTON *exits up* C, *closing the doors behind him.* SUSAN *wanders below the desk*)

MILLY (*moving to the fender and sitting*) She just has to hem the sleeves. I hope it fits. It's nice, Susie. Won't he be surprised!

SUSAN (*smiling*)  You don't think that perhaps we gave the game away?

MILLY.  No! (*Confiding delightedly*) He's expecting another one of these. (*She flicks the skirt of her black frock disdainfully*) I think—I really think I'll seem quite a different person.

SUSAN.  Let's hope not.

MILLY.  Please. I do so want to!

SUSAN.  Dearest . . . !

MILLY (*grimacing*)  Everyone has always been so very kind with me. Kind, kind, kind. Do you know why?

SUSAN (*dryly*)  Heavens, no.

MILLY.  Because they never see *me*. (*She rises and gives a gesture that sweeps with distaste from her neck to the floor*) They only see all this. (*She crosses to* C) But now, thanks to the signora——!

SUSAN (*moving to* L *of Milly; smiling*)  They'll see a gawky girl in white, and proceed to be quite horrid.

MILLY.  Oh. That isn't what I have in mind. (*She moves to* L *of the chaise. Graver, but not solemn, puzzling it out*) When a person's kind, just—sweetly kind: one somehow feels there isn't room for anything much else. Anything to grow, I mean. (*Feeling she has revealed too much, she dissembles with a gay smile*) Anything—surprising!

(GANASETA *enters up* C, *carrying a salver with a visiting card on it*)

SUSAN ⎫        ⎱ Yes, Ganaseta?
MILLY ⎬ (*together*) ⎰ (*She moves to Ganaseta*) The signora—does she
                                 need me?

GANASETA (*moving* C *and offering the salver*)  Permesso, signorina.

MILLY (*surprised*)  Oh . . . ? (*She takes the card and reads it*)

(SUSAN *moves to the downstage window and gazes out*)

Oh . . . (*More to herself than to Ganaseta; distressed*) Oh, no—I can't—I—(*She turns to say "No" to Ganaseta, then, realizing that this is not feasible, she turns to Susan*) Susie, do you think that you . . . ?

SUSAN (*moving up* L *of the desk*)  Who is it, dear?

MILLY.  Lord Mark.

SUSAN (*perturbed*)  Lord Mark? Oh. (*She crosses to* L *of Milly*) Then, of course, let me tell him that you're resting.

MILLY (*moving to the fireplace*)  I'll go up to the signora and—(*She checks*) Wait! (*She suddenly smiles with happy excitement and runs to Ganaseta*) Yes! Yes, Ganaseta—yes, of course I'll see him.

(GANASETA *nods and exits up* C, *leaving the doors open*)

SUSAN.  Are you sure you want to——?

MILLY (*cutting in; happily*)  Yes, Susie! Don't you understand?

SUSAN.  No. No, I don't think so.

MILLY.  But why else would he come here!

SUSAN.  Why *else*?

MILLY.  It can only be to tell us that Kate's accepted him!

Susan (*with a worried frown*) Are you sure, dear?

Milly. Certain! (*She hurries to the doors up* c *and speaks off*) Lord Mark!—how nice to see you. (*She holds out her hand*)

(Lord Mark *enters up* c *and takes Milly's hand formally*)

Lord Mark. Miss Theale.

(Milly *leads* Lord Mark *into the room.* Lord Mark *stands up* r *of the desk chair,* Milly *stands up* l *of it.*
Ganaseta *appears and closes the doors*)

Milly. When did you arrive? You remember Susan.

Lord Mark (*turning and giving Susan a formal nod*) Mrs Shepherd.

Susan (*equally formal*) Lord Mark. (*She moves to the fireplace*)

Milly. What's the news of Greece? How are Kate and Mrs Lowder?

Lord Mark (*politely, but not matching Milly's enthusiasm*) Quite well. They're both quite well.

Milly (*beaming*) Kate hasn't written. Not a word. I'm very vexed with her. (*She smiles through an awkward little pause*) Lord Mark, don't tease us—please. What have you got to tell us?

Lord Mark. I'm not sure I understand. (*He glances at Susan then back to Milly*) You said . . . ?

Milly. I hoped that—Nothing.

Lord Mark. Oh. (*He pauses and glances at Susan*) I wonder, Miss Theale—when I was here last month, I must confess I longed for a glimpse through your palazzo. If Mrs Shepherd would excuse us, perhaps on *this* occasion . . . ?

Milly. Unfortunately—(*to Susan*) Signora Fagioli will be waiting for me, won't she?

Susan. Yes. (*A token offer*) Would you like me to——?

Milly. No. (*To Lord Mark; with a helpless apologetic gesture as she moves up* c *to see him off*) It's—an awkward hour.

(Lord Mark *stonily refuses the cue*)

Are you *en route* for London? It was very good of you to drop in on us.

Lord Mark (*holding his ground*) Unpardonable at this hour, I appreciate. But I must ask for a moment alone with you, Miss Theale.

Milly (*firmly but gently*) I'm sorry.

Lord Mark (*curtly*) So am I. (*He crosses and looks out of the downstage window*) I must insist.

(Milly *is very angry, but the fact shows only in the set of her mouth and her carriage as she moves to the fireplace and nods to an extremely anxious* Susan *the fact that she may leave*)

Susan. Dearest, are you sure you . . . ?

Milly (*tight-lipped*) Yes.

(Susan *crosses and exits down* R, *closing the door behind her.* Milly *turns and faces Lord Mark across the room, without expression*)

Lord Mark (*moving down* C)  Mr Denver, I understand, has remained in Venice. (*He pauses*)

(Milly *does not reply*)

And not without a purpose—one might say, aspiration. But all this while he and Miss Croy have been secretly engaged.

Milly (*after a long, long motionless pause; gently*)  Dear Lord Mark . . . Has Kate refused you?

(Lord Mark *is silent*)

(*She crosses to him, touches his arm briefly in sympathy, then crosses slowly to* R *of the stool. With her back to him*)  Then, I see why . . .

Lord Mark.  Clearly, you do not. (*He takes a step towards Milly. For the first time his voice suggests that this interview is not without pain for him*)  Must I *explain* what they're banking on? Can't you piece it out?

Milly (*turning to him; kindly*)  Her refusal has been a very bitter disappointment. And unlooked for, unexpected; by me, too, I assure you—not yet quite understood.

Lord Mark.  I understand it.

Milly (*shaking her head; gravely*)  Not like this, Lord Mark.

Lord Mark (*with a step towards her*)  Would I invent the story for you?

Milly.  For yourself, perhaps.

Lord Mark.  Ah, no! Miss Croy was good enough to——

Milly (*interrupting sharply*)  No! You mustn't! (*Kindly, but with emphasis*)  Please understand: I cannot believe that Kate has told you this.

Lord Mark.  But she——

Milly (*cutting him off at once*)  If in fact she did so, for some strange, diplomatic reason of her own—why then, she will tell me. But I cannot accept it from anybody else. (*With simple and complete conviction*)  You see, it is a lie. And if you say—even hint—that Kate Croy is a liar, well—(*gently*) as her friend, Lord Mark, I could not be yours.

Lord Mark (*persevering, although his conviction is clearly shaken*)  I wonder if you know your friends.

Milly (*suddenly laughing merrily*)  Ohh . . . ! *You* don't, certainly! But not the least little bit about them! (*With a rush of sympathy*)  Forgive me, please. I didn't mean to laugh. And when you've been unhappy. Oh, it's too bad of me!

Lord Mark.  No.

Milly (*smiling warmly*)  We *are* friends, aren't we?

Lord Mark.  Yes.

Milly (*gaily*)  Yes!—I'm the friend you *do* know! (*She moves to the head of the chaise, mocking him fondly*)  That's because I'm easy.

LORD MARK (*moving up* C; *smiling ruefully*) At any rate, I give *her* up.

MILLY. You mean . . . ?

LORD MARK (*up* L *of the wing-chair*) I mean Miss Croy. Some day, you will have to explain her to me. Will you?

MILLY (*implying with a happy gesture the enormousness of the task*) Ohh . . . ! (*She moves up* R *of the wing-chair*) And, besides, that isn't fair: you've known them so much longer!

LORD MARK (*a thrown-away disclaimer*) Ah—my acquaintance with your other friend is very, very slight.

MILLY. Mr Denver? "Slight," indeed—for you to think him capable of—(*She catches herself up with a gay, apologetic smile*) I'm sorry!—all that's finished with. No—I referred to Kate and Mrs Lowder.

LORD MARK. I see. However, I shan't trouble you to explain the aunt. A massive subject; Mrs Lowder, but—how shall I put it?— she presents a silhouette that's quite sufficiently defined. On the other hand, look at Miss Croy and you'll soon note—the outline blurs; it shifts.

MILLY (*smiling; half-assenting*) Mmm . . . But, for me—(*confidently*) no longer. Kate is quite beautifully clear.

LORD MARK. Help me, then, some day. I've confidence in you; as you will have noticed . . . Good-bye, Miss Theale. (*He gives a polite nod, goes to the doors up* C *and opens them*)

MILLY. Good-bye. And I—(*with a step towards him; awkwardly*) I know that you meant well.

LORD MARK (*in the doorway*) If I could be as sure . . . But thank you. That has helped.

(LORD MARK *exits up* C, *closing the doors behind him. For a long moment,* MILLY *stands gazing at the doors without moving, then goes quickly to the bell-rope and pulls it. She waits, expressionless.*

PASQUALE *enters up* C)

MILLY. Pasquale——

(PASQUALE *moves up* R *of the desk*)

—when Mr Denver comes this evening, tell him I am not receiving.

PASQUALE (*after quelling his surprise*) La signorina padrona non riceve.

MILLY (*with a nod*) Please.

PASQUALE *bows and exits.* MILLY *crosses to the downstage window stool, sits, and stares down into the black water as—*

*the* CURTAIN *falls*

# ACT III

## SCENE I

SCENE—*The same. Three days later. Evening.*

*When the* CURTAIN *rises, the room is dark, the only light coming from the windows. The night sky is murky.* MILLY *is seated at the downstage window, looking down at the water. Her hair is loose. She is wearing a peignoir of dark brown chiffon and black lace. After a moment,* SUSAN'S *voice is heard off up* C.

SUSAN (*off*) I'll open it. Oh, very well. But no, don't bother to put it down; I'll take it. *Date qui la lampada*, Pasquale.

> (MILLY, *on hearing Susan's voice, turns and half rises as if to retreat, but sinks down on the seat again as the door opens.*
> PASQUALE *enters up* C, *carrying a lighted lamp. He holds the door open with his free hand.*
> SUSAN *enters up* C, *carrying a lighted lamp*)

(*She pauses and shivers*) Dear me, yes!—we'll need a fire. (*To Pasquale*) *Accendetela, per favore.*

PASQUALE (*crossing to the fireplace*) *Si, signora.* (*He puts the lamp on the right end of the mantelpiece, adjusts the wick, then takes matches from the mantelpiece and lights the fire*)

SUSAN (*putting her lamp on the table* R *of the arch*) I should have thought of it before. Three days of this weather, and the room not being used. (*She moves towards the downstage window*) I'll draw the— (*She suddenly sees Milly*) Milly . . . ! (*She moves quickly to her*) How long have you . . . ? Dearest—you're all right? (*She kneels and clasps Milly's hands*) But you're cold. Oh, Milly . . . ! (*She rises and attempts to hide her anguish with brisk nanny-like efficiency*) Straight back to bed with you.

MILLY (*guarded*) Where is he now, Susan?

SUSAN (*startled*) Who, dear?

MILLY (*with weary impatience*) The *dottore*—doctor—do you need his name?

SUSAN. Tacchini.

MILLY. Is the fire in here for him?

SUSAN (*moving to the doors up* C *and closing them*) *Andante pure,* Pasquale.

PASQUALE. *Ma la lampada, signora.*

SUSAN. I will do it. Thank you.

PASQUALE. *Si, signora.* (*He makes a little bow to Milly*) Signorina.

> (PASQUALE *exits down* R, *closing the door behind him*)

MILLY. Yes, let him sit in here, then; if it's comfort for you.

SUSAN (*moving to Milly*)  Now, come along to your room.

MILLY.  Not if he's still waiting. (*Coldly suspicious*) Is he?— is he there?

(SUSAN *moves below the right end of the desk, with a little cry of despair*)

SUSAN.  I don't know *where* he is, my dearest! (*She recovers control*) But Sir Luke Strett has the greatest confidence in him. (*She turns to Milly*)

MILLY (*vaguely*) Yes . . . well . . .

SUSAN.  *Let* him see you.

MILLY (*flatly*) But I did.

SUSAN.  Oh, darling Milly—once! And then, only for a moment.

MILLY.  Not again, Susan. What strength I have—I need myself. I can't attend to fools. For your sake, he may stay; only let him sit in here. (*With cold emphasis*) And do not talk about me. Please. Talk about—(*she loses interest. With a little shrug*) Ohh . . .

SUSAN.  Yes?

MILLY (*expressionless*) If you like, then—the price of vegetables.

(SUSAN, *hoping she is meant to laugh, tries to do so*)

SUSAN.  What a good idea! (*She rattles on in an attempt to establish a lighter mood*) Much more entertaining than his Venetian gossip. (*She crosses to the fireplace and takes a box of matches from the mantelpiece*) You may not realize it, but you've been so lucky: he only tries to doctor you—with me, he entertains! (*She crosses to the desk and lights the lamp on it*) And, in fact, you know, he hardly ever leaves us. Whatever can become of all his other patients? Anyone would think that you were royalty.

MILLY (*grimly*) He's waiting on events.

(SUSAN *gives a nervous little gasp and checks with the lighted match in her hand*)

SUSAN.  Ohh! (*Lightly*) Well, "waiting", certainly—poor man. Hovering outside your room, prowling through the halls. (*Having lit the lamp, she transfers it to the up* L *corner of the desk*) He bumps into me in doorways, in the sala, on the staircase. And always with that eager, intolerable smile! (*She puts the matches on the table* R *of the wing-chair*) Yes—the more I think about him, the more I think you're right. (*She turns, hoping for a response*)

(MILLY *is silent*)

Anyway . . . (*she moves below the wing-chair; hopefully*) Now that Sir Luke himself will soon be here . . .

MILLY (*tonelessly*) Keep me, Susan.

SUSAN.  Dearest?

MILLY.  Keep me, keep me. See me through.

(GANASETA *enters up* C)

GANASETA (*to Susan*) *Permesso, signora.*

SUSAN (*moving quickly to* L *of the wing-chair; with a little gesture*) No, not now.

GANASETA (*not understanding; moving to* R *of the desk chair*) C'e il signore Inglese.

MILLY (*sharply*) Who?

SUSAN. Milly!

MILLY (*peremptorily*) Who is it, Susan?

SUSAN. Milly—please!

MILLY. Ganaseta, *chi e?*

GANASETA (*nervously*) Signorina padrona . . . (*He looks at Susan*)

MILLY (*insistently*) Chi e?

GANASETA (*reluctantly*) Il signor Denver, *signorina*

MILLY (*rising and staring at Susan*) Then your fire was not for the *dottore.*

SUSAN (*moving below the desk; with a hard edge of desperation*) Don't deny me this. I need it. *I* need it, Milly. *I!*

MILLY (*after a pause; wry, but not rueful*) And once I promised you I'd be like carrying a feather. (*With an apologetic flick of the hand*) Susie . . . (*She crosses slowly towards the door down* R) But I believed he'd return to London.

SUSAN (*hard*) Oh—what you've believed!

(MILLY *stops below the chaise and turns to Susan, troubled*)

(*She shakes her head. Gently*) What you've believed, my dearest . . .

(MILLY *stares at Susan for a moment, then exits down* R, *leaving the door open*)

(*She turns and nods to Ganaseta*) Si.

GANASETA. *Si, signora.*

(GANASETA *exits up* C, *closing the doors behind him.* SUSAN, *in a small tight gesture, hammers the palm of one hand with the fist of the other and then, in control again, draws the window curtains and closes the door down* R

MERTON *enters up* C, *and closes the door behind him. He pauses at the door*)

SUSAN (*turning to Merton*) I've been so frightened.

MERTON. Is she dying . . . ?

(SUSAN *neither moves nor replies*)

(*He moves to* R *of the desk*) Thank you for sending Italo. I felt as if—— I've been waiting wretchedly.

SUSAN (*catching at it*) Wretchedly——?

MERTON. I've been waiting; I've been still. Still as a mouse. It seemed to me the only thing.

(SUSAN *moves to the head of the chaise. Without taking her eyes from* MERTON'S, *her hand suddenly flies to her face as her voice breaks with tears*)

SUSAN. I've been so frightened that you'd gone!

(MERTON *slowly and deliberately shakes his head*)

You *won't* go? You'll stay for me?

MERTON. Yes. Now. If I can't stay for Milly.

SUSAN (*moving below the table* C) She hasn't said your name. That is, not since—(*She drops her eyes from his and looks away down* R) As if she'd never known you.

MERTON (*turning away below the right end of the desk; quietly*) Well. She doesn't, then.

SUSAN (*turning to him*) I do. (*With a certain emphasis*) I mean, I always have. I've known.

MERTON (*turning to her; wondering*) You've known...?

SUSAN. Not everything. But you're here.

MERTON. So I may tell you...? (*He half-sighs*) Ohh...

SUSAN (*comfortably*) So we may help each other.

MERTON (*his fear dropping away*) You don't think badly of me?

SUSAN. No. (*She sits in the wing-chair*) She doesn't want to die. Think of her youth; of all she has. She lies there; she stiffens, and she tries to cling to it. (*She looks away from him*) There's not enough, though. Not enough. Now, there's not enough to cling to. I thank God...

MERTON (*wondering*) You thank God...?

SUSAN. That she's quiet.

MERTON. Quiet...?

SUSAN. More than quiet. Grim. (*She shakes her head*) But I couldn't —couldn't—! It would kill me if she spoke.

MERTON (*still at a loss*) If she...?

SUSAN. Spoke to me of how she clings. How she doesn't want it.

MERTON (*almost roughly*) How she doesn't want to die? Of course she doesn't want it!

(SUSAN *begins to weep quietly*)

(*He kneels beside her. Comforting*) Mrs Shepherd... Mrs Shepherd...

SUSAN (*weeping*) I don't know... I don't know... What harm have we done her...?

MERTON. *We*...?

SUSAN. I don't know... No-one ever will.

MERTON (*rising*) Would she see me?

SUSAN (*her tears stopped; staring at him*) Would you—like it?

MERTON. No.

SUSAN. Ah——

MERTON. Not as you describe her——

SUSAN. —then...!

MERTON. —but, if she could bear it, I'd do anything.

SUSAN (*rising and moving to* L *of the chaise*) There's one thing you could do. There's only that one thing. (*She turns as if hoping he will name it*) I think you know what it is.

Merton (*moving below the wing-chair*) First, please, let me understand. You believe she's dying?

Susan. Oh—! (*She sits on the chaise, with her hands clasped and her head
down*)

Merton. But the doctor, what does *he*——?

Susan. Tacchini? Very kind. But she . . . (*She gives a hopeless shrug*)

Merton. I meant—I thought that Sir Luke Strett——?

(Susan *finds her handkerchief and wipes away her tears*)

Susan (*quickly*) I wired him. Oh, yes—it's Sir Luke who's kept
me going. He answered like an angel, and he'll come like one. By
Thursday; Thursday afternoon.

Merton. That's something.

Susan. Something—yes. She likes him. Will you do it if *he* asks
you to?

Merton. Will I . . . ?

Susan (*rising*) Will you deny it to her if he thinks that it will help?

Merton. Will I deny what, Mrs Shepherd?

Susan. Why, what Lord Mark told Milly.

Merton. And that is . . . ?

Susan. I thought you knew——!

Merton. I knew he must have seen her, yes.

Susan. But surely, then—! (*She decides not to persist*) Lord Mark
said that all this while you and Miss Croy have been engaged.

(Merton *flinches and moves up* r *of the desk*)

Merton (*almost savagely*) All *what* while?

Susan (*gently*) I'm only repeating what he told her, Mr Denver.

Merton (*catching himself up and turning back to her*) Forgive me.
Of course, I knew; I guessed. I saw him late that evening, after
coming here and being turned away. Only saw him, mind you—in
the piazza, through the window of a café—*Florian's*. But to see him
was enough: enough to know why he had come.

Susan. He can't have meant to harm her.

Merton (*with a step towards her*) Nonetheless, he must have
known—even on his first visit—he must have known, he must have
*seen* the weakness of her hold on life.

Susan (*grimly*) He knew. He knew.

Merton (*studing her face*) On his first visit, can you mean—he
proposed to her *because* . . . ?

Susan. Oh, just because—of course.

Merton. What sort of brute is he, then?

Susan. He knew what you have known.

(*The implied accusation staggers* Merton)

Merton. What *I* have known! (*He steps back*) But, I—I——!

Susan (*holding up her hand to stop him; kindly*) But you—*you* walked
on tip-toe. Now it's too late for that. (*She takes a step towards him*)

If Sir Luke asks it, as something that may help him save her, will you give Milly a denial?

MERTON. You're certain she believes?

SUSAN (*appealing to their whole situation*) Certain . . . !

MERTON (*accepting this*) Yes . . . Do *you*?

SUSAN (*after a brief pause; rather stiffly*) What I believe depends on your action, Mr Denver. (*She moves to the fireplace*) If, to save her life, you consent to a denial—(*she turns to him and relaxes*) I promise I'll believe you right down to the ground.

MERTON. No. (*He moves to L of the wing-chair*) What is it, please, that you believe at this very moment?

SUSAN (*mildly*) By now, I thought you knew. (*As if it is unimportant*) I believe what Lord Mark said. I've believed it ever since the day you came to Venice.

MERTON (*hushed*) Why?—how?

SUSAN. Maud Lowder told me.

MERTON (*astonished*) Mrs Lowder!

SUSAN. Oh, only that her niece cared for you, of course. But, from that, it was quite simple.

MERTON. Simple?

SUSAN. Why, to follow Miss Croy's—system, scheme.

(MERTON *looks astonished*)

Oh, yes. I've even *helped* her.

MERTON (*bewildered*) You've helped Kate?

SUSAN. With poor, dear, trusting Maud. From me, you see—it was convincing; she never questioned it. Little bits of tittle-tattle: things you'd said to Milly, and——

MERTON (*cutting in; with a step towards her*) Things I'd said to her?

SUSAN (*surprised he has not understood*) Things I invented—lies. I'd whisper them to Maud. Oh, pretending, of course, that they'd come to me from Milly.

MERTON. But why?

SUSAN (*crossing below Merton to R of the wing-chair*) So that Maud wouldn't guess—wouldn't stop what Miss Croy planned. You *had* to be persuaded to stay on alone with us! Who but Miss Croy could do it?

(MERTON *stares at her*)

No—please, don't look at me like that. (*She looks away*) You think me very wicked. But you were all my hope.

MERTON. You never thought of telling Milly.

SUSAN. As Lord Mark did, you mean? (*She moves a step up R. Grimly*) I had no choice, Mr Denver. (*She turns to him. Harshly*) Besides, I thought Kate Croy would lose. In time, I thought she'd lose you.

(MERTON *stares at her*)

(*She looks away. Almost whispering*) I didn't see how you could help but love my Milly.

(MERTON *moves below the desk*)

MERTON (*mumbling*) But Kate and I—Kate's given me—(*He turns and shakes his head*) I couldn't. It's too late.

SUSAN. Like her aunt, like dearest Maud—with twenty other *splendid* qualities, she's the least bit brutal.

MERTON. (*hesitantly*) You may think——

SUSAN (*cutting in*) And you are not.

MERTON. But, Mrs Shepherd——

SUSAN (*cutting in*) Are you? (*She takes a step towards him. Insisting*) *Are* you?

MERTON (*as if ashamed*) No.

SUSAN (*immediately*) Then tell Milly that it isn't true. Tell Milly. Will you?

(*They face each other. Neither moves*)

*Please!*

(MERTON *turns slowly to the downstage window*)

(*She watches him intently. In a small voice; bitterly ashamed*) I could force you.

(MERTON *turns*)

Knowing what I know . . .

MERTON. Mrs Shepherd . . .

SUSAN (*quickly*) Say you will. Say "yes".

MERTON (*gently explaining*) If I tell Milly, it must be because I mean it.

(MILLY *enters up* C, *leaving the doors open. She is wearing a white dress and carries a substantial shawl of dark brown wool, half-concealed behind her*)

SUSAN (*moving to* R *of the wing-chair*) Milly . . . !

MILLY (*smiling at Susan*) Susan, dear. (*She gives Merton a tranquil smile*) Good evening, Mr Denver. (*She moves to* L *of the wing-chair*) Has Susan been telling you . . . ?

(MERTON *and* SUSAN *exchange a look*)

(*Still smiling, she studies Merton's face*) No, I see she's been too modest. (*She turns to Susan; happily, not coy*) He's in the music-room; he's waiting. (*To Merton*) Susan has found an admirer, you see. Or, rather, he's found her. His name's Tacchini. He's a doctor. (*To Susan*) I said I'd find you for him.

SUSAN (*very concerned*) I can't—I can't *let* you——!

MILLY (*deliberately, lightly mistaking her meaning*) You're quite right; I shouldn't tease. (*She moves to Merton*) I've had a chill—oh, nothing much! Doctor Tacchini came for me. I do suspect, though, it's for Susie's *beaux yeux* that he returns. (*To Susan*) Why not join him, dear?—just in case I'm not mistaken. (*She decides not to press and moving towards the head of the chaise, feigns indifference*) But perhaps you think that he's a nuisance, so don't let me—(*For no apparent reason she stumbles slightly and grasps the head of the chaise for support*)

SUSAN (*with a step towards Milly; with an involuntary gasp*) Milly ...!

MILLY (*straightening; calmly and lightly*) Don't let me bully you.

SUSAN (*crossing above the wing-chair to* C) Mr Denver and I have—(*She half turns to Merton*) I've been asking something of him.

MILLY (*casually*) Oh, yes, Susie?—what?

SUSAN. Like your chill, dear—nothing much. And, in fact, I knew the answer. (*To Merton. Easily; a statement*) The answer's "Yes". It has to be. (*To Milly. Immediately*) Stay by the fire, now, where it's warm.

(SUSAN *exits up* C, *closing the doors behind her*)

MERTON (*moving down* L *of the desk*) Don't wear black any more. The dress is lovely.

MILLY. Isn't it! But thank heaven you said so quickly! (*She puts the shawl around her shoulders*) Now I can put this back on. If you noticed, that's why Susie was upset when I came in. (*She moves to* L *of the wing-chair. Defending herself*) It was on right to the door. (*A forthright admission*) I thought it might spoil the effect.

MERTON. The effect was perfect.

MILLY. Thanks. Don't look too closely, though. I had to powder. My nose was—! (*She moves quickly above the desk*) Have you had a cold? Do be careful, please. But now the weather's changed, of course, you'll return to London.

MERTON. And to sunshine, do you mean?

MILLY (*laughing*) No ...! (*Grave but serene*) I mean that—well, that Venice isn't—(*she shakes her head*) can't be now, as it has been these past few weeks.

(MERTON *turns, parts the curtains of the downstage window and looks out*)

MERTON. It's suddenly become a Venice all of evil. When just three days ago ...! Now—see?—the sky's like ink; and so low you feel you could reach up and dip a pen in it. (*He looks down at the canal*) The gondoliers are huddled under the archways—stranded, wageless. Better that than working, though, in rain like this: it lashes. (*He turns and crosses above Milly to* L *of the wing-chair*) But coming here, I was astounded when I cut through the piazza. Even now, you know, it seems that half of Venice gathers there! Oh—sheltered, of course, in the arcades and galleries. (*He closes in behind Milly a little*) Some day you must come—you must see the piazza. I'll be very stern with you, and I'll force you out. Into the drawing-room of Europe. That's how I think of it. It's so hugely elegant. But desolate today—wide open to the storm. And bewildered—by its reverse of fortune.

Milly (*turning to him; kindly and gently*) Don't think of staying. I thought that you had gone. But when I heard this evening—well, don't stay for me. That's all. (*a pause*) There's so little need of it. Although, I must admit—I would like more about your mother. Do you remember telling me?—the lady-copyist.

Merton (*nodding*) The National Gallery—the copyists you were watching.

Milly (*crossing to the fireplace*) I wish I'd spoken to them. I would have liked to try to—to get into their lives.

Merton (*moving to* r *of the desk and turning to her; surprised and amused*) But why?

Milly (*sharing his amusement*) I don't know exactly! (*She pauses briefly*) I suppose because they were safe. They were secure. (*Explaining*) You see, those pictures on the walls—those great Titians and those Turners—they seemed to swirl all round about me. Dazzling; frightening. (*She smiles and shrugs*) I was too weak for them. (*She sits on the left side of the chaise, facing front*) But if I'd been a careful lady-copyist—(*she suddenly holds out her right hand at arm's length*) with my life there—just there—safely in front of me. In reach. (*She concentrates on her hand*) There it is. And all you do is study it, stick at it, and stick and stick and stick. (*She drops her arm*)

Merton. Had you spoken to them—to the lady-copyists, you'd have learned that they were dreaming—well, not of safely "sticking to it", but, rather, of some—oh, impossible adventure!

Milly. Yes . . . How I hope, then, that they find it. Just as I found mine.

Merton. Your adventure . . . ?

Milly (*looking at him with loving happiness*) My adventure. Mine was a quiet room—sitting in a quiet room, with you. (*After a brief pause*) Good-bye.

(*Tears have rushed to* Merton's *eyes and he tries to speak, taking a step towards her*)

Merton. Milly, let me tell you . . . Try to tell you . . .

Milly (*rising*) Please—I promise you: I don't need it now . . . Good-bye . . .

Merton (*whispering*) Good-bye . . .

(Merton *looks into Milly's face for a moment then turns abruptly and exits up* c, *closing the doors behind him.* Milly *moves slowly and carefully to the desk. Her face is radiant. She sits, takes pen and paper and begins to write.*

Susan *enters down* r)

Susan. Dearest . . . ?

Milly (*turning to Susan and smiling; after a pause*) He liked my frock.

Susan (*closing the door and moving to the head of the chaise*) He's gone, then?

Milly. Yes. I'm writing to him.

SUSAN (*moving between the chaise and the wing-chair; puzzled*) Writing . . . ?

MILLY (*smiling*) Oh, we shan't meet again.

SUSAN (*anxiously*) But, I could call—could send Pasquale——

MILLY (*shaking her head*) I'm writing now in case I can't—(*She checks herself*) The letter is for later on. He'll read it in London. On Christmas Day. With Kate.

(SUSAN *looks away*)

(*Sensing Susan's anguish, she speaks with comforting cheerfulness*) Susie, where's that lovely silk embroidery you do?

SUSAN. Last night, I—In your room, I think.

MILLY (*looking down at her letter*) After this one, I've another; for New York; it must be—if you wouldn't mind?—it must be witnessed.

SUSAN. Yes.

MILLY (*happily*) So why not fetch your work in here?

SUSAN (*looking at Milly and trying to smile*) To keep you company? Of course. (*She moves to the doors up* C)

MILLY. And Susie . . . ?

(SUSAN *stops*)

SUSAN (*without turning*) Yes . . . ?

MILLY (*lightly but carefully*) Mrs Lowder—*all* our friends—must know how more than kind he's been.

SUSAN. Yes.

MILLY. Oh, thank you, Susie!

SUSAN *exits up* C, *closing the doors behind her.* MILLY *returns to her letter as*—

*the* CURTAIN *falls*

SCENE 2

SCENE—*The same. An afternoon in late December.*

*When the* CURTAIN *rises, the room is empty. The fire is burning. The day is clear. After a moment* GANASETA *enters up* C *and stands aside.* MERTON *enters up* C.

GANASETA. *Vado a dire alle signore che lei e qui.*

MERTON (*moving* C) *Per favore.*

(GANASETA *exits up* C, *closing the doors behind him.* MERTON *stands still for a moment, letting his eyes roam over the room, sombrely, as if re-discovering it, then he takes from his pocket a very thick, long envelope, glances dispassionately at it, absently taps it on his hand as he surveys the room again, this time purposefully. His eyes settle on the desk. He moves quickly to it, drops the envelope on it and then immediately moves to the up-stage window and gazes out.*

*KATE enters quietly down* R *and stands in silence for a few moments, looking at Merton)*

KATE (*smiling*) We've been in Venice five long hours.

(MERTON *turns and smiles gravely*)

(*She closes the door*) When we landed, I had hoped you might be there to greet us.

MERTON. But would that have been in keeping——?

(KATE *tilts her chin with a puzzled smile*)

—with our wonderful system, Kate.

KATE. You don't want to take your rebound at a rush. I understand.

MERTON. I don't want to *appear* to.

(KATE *gives Merton a rueful glance, then moves to the fireplace*)

KATE. Oh, we're infernally clever, you and I! (*She longs to go to him but there is something in Merton's tender gravity that holds her back*) Has it been very terrible?

MERTON (*moving to* L *of the desk*) Milly's death, you mean—her dying? (*He thinks for a moment*) Well, yes—very terrible to me. (*He turns to the downstage window*) But I only had the faintest, briefest glimpse of it, you know. You should ask Mrs Shepherd.

KATE. Well . . .

MERTON. She's been magnificent.

KATE (*with a small edge of irony*) "Magnificent?" (*With conviction*) Milly was.

MERTON (*turning to look at her*) Oh, you don't know . . . !

KATE (*with a surprised little smile*) She was my friend.

MERTON. And you were sure of it.

KATE (*puzzled*) Of course.

MERTON. If you don't think Mrs Shepherd has been magnificent, what of Lord Mark—do you think *he* has been, Kate?

KATE (*bewildered*) Lord Mark? I haven't seen him.

MERTON. But you know that he saw Milly after leaving you in Greece?

KATE. Yes.

MERTON. Then do you know the rest?

KATE. What rest?

MERTON. His visit killed her, killed your friend.

KATE (*shocked*) His visit . . . ? But our letters haven't told us *that*.

MERTON. No? She simply gave up after it; she gave up caring.

KATE. *Why* . . . ?

MERTON (*cold and strong*) He informed her that we have been secretly engaged.

KATE (*incredulously*) What . . . ? (*Strongly*) But he doesn't know it!

E

MERTON. *She* did, when he'd left her. (*He turns to the window*) And how?—if not from you?

KATE (*with a step towards him*) Couldn't you have told her . . . ? That it wasn't true, I mean.

(MERTON *does not reply*)

(*She moves to* R *of the desk*) You must have tried? But *surely* . . . !

MERTON. I didn't have the chance.

KATE (*staring at him*) She wouldn't see you?

MERTON (*shaking his head*) After his visit . . .

KATE. All this while?

MERTON. Once. She saw me once.

KATE. And then——?

MERTON. She was already dying.

KATE. But to save her——!

MERTON (*turning*) If I had told her, Kate, I'd have stuck to it.

KATE (*searching his face, but taking a step away*) You mean—you would have chucked me?

MERTON (*sitting on the downstage window stool; reluctantly*) What else could I have done?

KATE (*with wonder*) You're in love with her!

MERTON (*roughly*) With a dead girl! (*He turns away*) Well, say so, if you want to!

(KATE, *relieved, moves to Merton for the first time, and touches his shoulder*)

KATE. Forgive me. (*She prompts him*) When she saw you, then—(*she withdraws her hand*) you denied nothing?

MERTON. She wouldn't even let me try. Oh, she was merciful.

KATE. Then why?—why let you come? (*Without irony*) Was it just once more to look at you? Tell me what she said.

MERTON. That I mustn't wait.

KATE. Only that?

MERTON. That was really all. And in perfect kindness.

KATE (*looking away*) Mustn't wait to see her die.

MERTON. Do you remember telling me, she wouldn't "smell" of drugs, wouldn't "taste" of medicine? Well, she didn't, Kate.

KATE (*eagerly*) So that it was almost happy?

MERTON (*rising and crossing to* L *of the wing-chair*) I won't try to tell you now what it was for me.

KATE (*moving below the desk*) Did she show any feeling—any feeling, I mean, of having been misled—by us?

MERTON (*moving above the wing-chair; looking away*) She showed only her beauty. Her beauty and her strength.

KATE. Her *strength* . . . ? (*Musing*) Yes . . . That was *our* strength, too: that she loved you with passion. (*She sighs*) Ah, then, thank God . . . !

(MERTON *looks at Kate*)

Thank God. She was at peace with you.

MERTON (*moving* C; *murmuring*) Oh, "peace". . . !

KATE. The peace of having loved.

MERTON (*looking intently at her*) Is that so peaceful, Kate?

KATE. Of having used her passion. She wanted nothing else. She had it all. It's what I've hoped. (*She smiles serenely at him*) It's what we've worked for—both of us. You needn't say: I know now we've succeeded.

MERTON (*turning away; murmuring*) Ohh . . . !

KATE (*with a gentle little smile for his distaste*) I won't make odious speculations, but I know we haven't failed. It's not in vain she loved you, or in vain that you love me. (*She moves to Merton, reaching for him*)

(MERTON *moves to the fireplace*)

(*Down* R *of the desk*) *Do* you?

MERTON. Yes, I love you. (*He takes a small envelope from his pocket*) It's because I love you that I've brought you this. (*He holds out the letter*)

KATE. Is it to you?

(MERTON *nods*)

And it's from her. (*She crosses to* L *of him*) You look troubled; you're not well.

MERTON. Oh—well enough.

KATE (*puzzling out his face*) And yet I see—I think—you hate what you're doing.

MERTON (*curtly*) It isn't quite so simple. (*He looks at the envelope*) The letter is from Milly. (*He brusquely offers the letter to Kate*)

KATE (*taking the letter*) But it isn't opened!

MERTON. No.

KATE. How long, then, have you had it?

MERTON (*crossing to the head of the chaise*) Four days.

KATE. Four days!

MERTON. Since Christmas Eve.

KATE. Christmas Eve? But Milly died——

MERTON (*cutting in abruptly*) Yes. She was already dead.

KATE. She'd written and then kept it.

MERTON (*nodding*) For Christmas. Yes.

KATE. The season of gifts. (*She holds the letter out to him*) You have your proof.

MERTON (*ignoring the letter; sharply*) My proof!—of what?

KATE (*pressing the letter into his hand*) Why, of the beauty with which you have been loved by her, my dear.

MERTON (*looking at the letter*) This was to be *your* proof; I want to give you one. I want to let you see—to have—something I feel sacred.

KATE (*frowning*) I don't understand.

MERTON. I asked myself how I could—what proof—what sacrifice—what *symbol*, then, if that's the word . . . Your coming to me

—to my rooms. (*He holds out the letter. Pleading*) Kate, let this be a symbol of what that has meant to me.

KATE. You're afraid of yourself. But *why* . . . ?

MERTON. Kate . . . ! Please . . . !

KATE (*wrenching her eyes from his face and looking at the letter*) You absolutely want me to?

MERTON. I absolutely want you to.

KATE. To do—what I like with?

MERTON. Yes. Save only that—what she says must be between us.

KATE (*nodding and taking the letter*) To hold it is to know.

MERTON (*frowning; impatiently*) Oh, I *know*!

KATE. Then, if we both do . . . ! (*She stoops and throws the letter on the fire then crosses to R of the desk*) You'll have the details from New York.

(MERTON *stiffens to prevent himself from snatching the letter out of the fire, and stands, his hands gripping the mantelpiece, watching it burn. He has not heard Kate*)

(*She turns to him after a pause*) But, my dear, I said, you'll have the details from New York. (*She reassures him with a troubled frown*) Of *how* she has made you rich; to what amount. (*With a little smile*) I trust her.

MERTON (*moving to R of the chaise; abstracted*) Those. Oh, why, they're here.

KATE (*wide-eyed and eager*) You have them?

MERTON (*impatiently; without interest*) Details? Yes.

KATE. But how?

MERTON. Mr Someone-or-other, the—trustee—executor—head of whatever legal firm handled her affairs. (*He sits on the right side of the chaise*)

KATE (*moving below the wing-chair*) Yes?

MERTON (*as if mildly surprised she does not know*) He's still in Venice; he's been here a week or so.

KATE. You've seen him?

MERTON (*suddenly almost jovial*) No, indeed not! I've avoided that, at least!

KATE. But, then . . . ?

MERTON. Oh—a thumping great envelope left for me at my lodgings. The *padrona* took it in. (*He smiles broadly*) And squeezed it underneath my door!

KATE. Oh . . . ?

MERTON. The blasted thing got wedged there! I couldn't open it.

KATE (*after a brief pause; warily*) You couldn't open . . . ?

MERTON. Oh, the door, I mean.

KATE. And the envelope——?

MERTON. Well, at last I coaxed it out. (*He beams*) And I say, you know—what luck!—The seal hadn't even cracked.

KATE. Hadn't it . . . ? Well . . . ! (*She pauses and moves below the desk. With some edge*) Then does the "symbol" of your love for me not include *that* letter?

(MAUD *enters up* C, *leaving the doors open. She exudes portentous sympathy*)

MAUD. Ahh . . . !

(MERTON *rises.* KATE *moves to the downstage window*)

You poor, dear thing! Dear Mr Denver!

MERTON (*with something between a nod and a bow*) Mrs Lowder.

MAUD. Our little dove, then—as Kate calls her—has folded her wings.

MERTON (*inwardly wincing; formally*) Folded them; yes.

MAUD (*moving to* L *of the wing-chair*) Unless it's more true that she has spread them but the wider. For a flight, we trust, to some greater happiness.

MERTON (*warning her with a little frown and a slight turn away*) Greater; yes; exactly.

MAUD (*to Kate; with more reserve*) Susan will have tea upstairs. She's still— (*She turns to Merton, oozing sympathy*) But, then, you understand: you share her grief just as you've shared her long and cruel ordeal.

MERTON (*a stiff denial*) As between what Mrs Shepherd and what I have had to——

MAUD (*moved by his modesty, but having none of it*) She's told me—she's told me everything! Your sweet devotion . . .

KATE (*warning Merton with a look not to reveal too much; firmly*) You did stay.

MAUD. Right to the end . . . !

MERTON. Oh, well, yes—I *had* to stay. How else could I show— (*blurting it out almost angrily*) how well—how awfully well I'd meant? (*He moves up* R)

MAUD (*moved almost to tears*) How well you'd meant? Dear friend, dear friend, you showed us more than that.

KATE (*to Merton; fearing that Maud's sentiment may prompt another denial; matter-of-factly*) I wonder only that they *let* you stay.

MAUD (*quickly and indignantly*) Kate!

KATE. So many weeks, I mean.

MAUD. Kate Croy—how could you!

KATE. I refer to his employers—to his paper; no-one else.

MAUD (*deflated*) Ohh. (*She dismisses the trivial point*) Well, they've had to do without him. The clever creature.

MERTON (*with a grim little smile*) Quite.

KATE (*with a step towards Merton*) You don't mean . . . ?

MERTON (*moving to* L *of the chaise*) Oh, yes—they sacked me.

KATE. No!

MAUD. I cancel my subscription. (*Pleased with herself*) There!

MERTON. That's very handsome.

MAUD (*beaming*) Sweet of you. (*Briskly*) Remind me, Kate. (*She moves to Merton*) Now I must go to Susan. But I wanted—(*her hand on his arm*) you mustn't doubt; I'm *with* you, you poor dear.

MERTON. Thank you, Mrs Lowder.

MAUD (*preparing for another flight of sentiment*) Ah, when I look at you and think of how she must have longed to live . . .

KATE. To live? Of course she did.

(MAUD, *thrown by having her histrionic pause filled, gives Kate a cross look and moves to the doors up* C)

MAUD. Well, why in pity shouldn't she, with everything to fill her world? (*Having ticked Kate off, she turns to Merton*) Oh, the mere money of her, the darling! If it isn't too disgusting at such a time to mention that.

(MAUD *exits up* C, *closing the doors behind her*)

KATE. Is it? Is it too disgusting?

MERTON. Oh, yes—your details.

KATE. Well . . . ?

MERTON (*moving to* R *of the desk; hard*) First, please: I asked you, but you know, you didn't answer.

KATE. What?

MERTON. How did he know that we're engaged?

KATE. Lord Mark. I see! You think I *told* him!

MERTON (*insisting*) How did he know?

KATE (*strongly*) He can't have known. It was a guess. If he had "known", as you say, how could Milly have convinced him?

MERTON. Milly . . . ?

KATE. How could she have convinced him it was her you really loved?

MERTON. Milly convinced him?

KATE. Yes. He wrote to us. If you'd only asked yourself: *why* would I have told him? His guess—his mere guess nearly cost us— (*with a little smile*) well, what . . . ?

(MERTON *moves to* L *of the wing-chair*)

Please, may I know now? (*She moves to* L *of the desk*)

MERTON. But if Milly hadn't died . . . (*He looks at her*) *That* would have cost us, wouldn't it?

KATE. Cost me, you mean. For you'd have married her.

(*For a moment they stare at each other*)

Well, yes. For a while.

MERTON (*moving up* R *of the desk*) For a while? But you once told me that you'd wait for me for ever.

KATE. And I also told you that there'd be no need.

MERTON (*flatly*) Ahh.

KATE (*frowning*) What do you mean?

MERTON. How long were you thinking that you might allow her?

(*He moves down* C *and wheels to her. Quickly*) How long before arranging that she—(*he shrugs*) somehow—stumbled on the truth?

KATE (*moving down* LC) Then I understand. If you thought for one moment that I'd engineered her death—oh, then I understand why you look at me as if . . . (*With an involuntary little grimace she looks away from him*) But what I *don't* understand is *how*: how you could have thought it. (*She turns to him*) How, my dear . . . ? (*She moves to him*)

(MERTON *moves to* L *of the chaise.* KATE *checks below the right end of the desk*)

MERTON (*in weary, surly self-distaste*) Please, Kate. (*He sits on the left side of the chaise. Perfunctorily*) Then, as you say, he guessed.

KATE. He guessed. You do believe me?

MERTON. Why not? If Susan Shepherd guessed, why not Lord Mark as well?

KATE (*startled*) Mrs Shepherd? She's said nothing!

MERTON (*bitterly*) Oh, no! She's been "protecting" me!

KATE (*with a small, ironic, tender smile*) You please people; you please all of us.

MERTON (*roughly*) What sort of a brute of a humbug, then, have I become? (*He points perfunctorily to the desk*) The envelope is there.

(KATE *moves to the desk, picks up the envelope, and after a quick speculative glance at Merton, opens it. There is a letter on a single sheet accompanied by a number of corroborative documents.* KATE *reads the letter and then, still holding it, spreads the documents on the desk. Finally, she puts down the letter and turns, smiling, to* MERTON, *who has been motionless, watching her*)

KATE. I didn't hesitate this time to break your seal.

MERTON. It isn't mine.

KATE. Ours, then.

MERTON. Oh, no. Please. *Theirs.* We might have sent it back intact. (*He smiles farewell to this possibility with a sigh*) However!— well and good.

KATE (*motionless and careful*) "Sent it back?"

MERTON. It's too late, now—well, ideally. They'll see we know.

KATE. You don't.

MERTON. To send it back unopened would have been the ideal way.

KATE (*moving* C; *with an incredulous little gasp*) But, my dear man— aren't you curious?

MERTON. No. And please don't tell me.

KATE (*gently mocking*) You have to do it with your eyes tight shut?

MERTON. Do what?

KATE (*moving to* L *of him*) Why, send it back to them. (*Strongly*) Refuse Milly's wish.

MERTON. I'll refuse it only if I have your consent.

KATE. Mine——?

MERTON. Yes.

KATE. —My consent? Why?

MERTON. We've done this together.

KATE. Done it! Yes! Why now consent to throw it all away?

MERTON (*turning away; with strong emotion*) Because—quite simply —I can't bear it.

KATE (*staring at him*) Something's happened——

MERTON (*turning to her*) Kate!

KATE. —But what?

MERTON. Say I've your consent.

KATE. What has happened?

MERTON. Say I have it.

KATE. *Why?*

MERTON (*pleading*) We owe this to our feelings for ourselves and for each other. If we marry now, marry without her money, that will, somehow—don't you see?—right all we've done that's wrong. It will make us——

KATE (*cutting in*) What has changed you?

MERTON. Nothing.

KATE. Why, then, are you afraid?

MERTON (*evading the question with angry impatience*) Will you consent, Kate? Answer me!

(KATE *turns sharply from him, then moves slowly to the desk, leans on it, gazes down at the documents and smiles*)

KATE. It's worthy of her. It's what she was herself.

MERTON. Magnificent . . . ?

KATE. Magnificent . . . But you're afraid of knowing all that she has done: you know more now than you can bear. You're afraid— it's wonderful!—to be in love with Milly.

MERTON (*concealing how close he is to tears; turning away*) I never was in love with her.

KATE. Not while she lived; not while she lived for you. The change came, I should think, the last time that she saw you. She released you then, "died" for you that you might understand her. And from that hour you *did*. Her selflessness—her selfless, boundless generosity. You understand, and you're afraid. (*She lightly flicks the papers*) She did this for *us*. She did it knowing—*wanting* you and me to be together.

(MERTON *rises and faces her*)

I used to call her a dove—(*with an ironic smile*) as Aunt Maud remembered. Well, she stretched out her wings. They reached. They cover us . . . (*She flinches*) Oh, yes—*I*'m afraid, too.

MERTON. Then you mean . . . ?

KATE. That I do consent? (*She moves to R of the desk*) I consent to nothing until you've answered me. *Are* you in love with her?

MERTON. No . . . !

KATE. With her memory?

MERTON. Kate . . . !

KATE (*moving to* L *of him*) Oh, don't pretend you couldn't be. I could, in your place. Is her memory your love? Do you want another?

MERTON. I'll marry you tomorrow.

KATE. That isn't what I asked!

MERTON. We'll be as we were, before . . .

KATE. Will we . . . ? (*She gazes into his face, then turns away*) Never . . . ! (*She moves to the doors up* C, *opens them and turns*) No, my dear . . .

KATE *closes the doors and exits as—*

*the* CURTAIN *falls*

# FURNITURE AND PROPERTY LIST

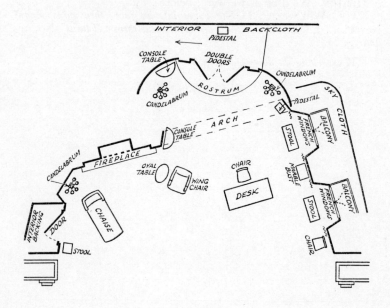

## ACT I

### Scene 1

*On stage:* Small stool with terra-cotta velvet top, to match the curtains (down R)

Chaise-longue, upholstered in light brown velvet. *On it:* cushion

Club fender, upholstered in green leather

*In hearth:* fire-grate of coals, fire-dogs, fire-irons

*On mantelpiece:* large, black marble clock, 2 Baroque figures, 2 dark iron candlesticks, 2 books, 2 boxes matches

*Over mantelpiece:* heavy dark tapestry

High-back wing-chair upholstered in green brocade. *On it:* cushion

Small oval table (C) *On it:* long green wool cover, with green silk cover and grey lace cover over it, small oil-lamp

Console table with green marble top (R of arch) *On it:* green plaster bust of bearded man

Console table (R of doors) *On it:* long ochre velvet cover, small black iron figurine

Desk, painted green with gold ornament. *On it:* green folding blotter, writing-paper, envelopes, Maud's green leather writing-case containing writing-paper and letter from Lady Danby; large inkstand, pen-tray with pens, red *Baedecker*, guide-book, small roller blotter, wood box, Wedgwood dish, standing calendar, tall silver inkpot

Desk chair, upholstered in terra-cotta velvet

Pedestal (L of arch) *On it:* terra-cotta bust of woman

Long stool (at upstage window)

Long stool (at downstage window)

Ornate console table (between windows) *On it:* brown statuette of Venus de Milo

Long, velvet terra-cotta coloured curtains hanging on brass rods with rings at both windows

Braided tie-backs on hooks beside curtains

Braid and gilt bell-rope R of fireplace

Ornate gilt mirror (on wall down L)

Small upright chair (down L)

*On landing:* green pedestal. *On it:* green plaster bust of woman

Carpet on floor RC

Doors closed

Downstage leaf of downstage window open

Fire off

Lamp off

*Off stage:* Leather-bound book (MILLY)
   Silver salver. *On it:* visiting card (GANASETA)
   Hat (LORD MARK)

*Personal:* MILLY: long, double rope of pearls
   SUSAN: fob watch, handkerchief, handbag, gloves
   MAUD: handbag. *In it:* gloves
   KATE: handbag
   LORD MARK: wallet. *In it:* lira note

### SCENE 2

*Strike:* Books and Maud's letter from desk

*Set:* Tall, ornate six-branch standard candelabrum with 6 tall candles and shades (L of doors up C)
   Matching candelabrum (R of fireplace)
   Oil lamp (on table between windows)
   *On left end of desk:* box with 6 candles
   *On table R of wing-chair:* embroidery on round frame for Susan, with silks, needle, scissors, etc., in sewing-bag

Doors closed

Windows closed

Window curtains closed
Candelabrum L of door, all candles lit
Candelabrum R of fireplace, 3 candles lit
Oil-lamp L, lit
Oil-lamp on table C: lit
Fire out

*Off stage:*  Taper, with self-contained battery (GANASETA)
          Matching candelabra, but without candles or shades (MILLY)
          2 lighted oil-lamps (GANASETA)
          Feather fan (MAUD)

# ACT II

## SCENE 1

*Strike:*  Table-lamps from table L, and mantelpiece

*Move:*  Candelabrum down L to R of table R of doors up C and fit with
      shades

*Set:*  *On desk:* writing-paper, envelopes, pen, 4 envelopes containing tips,
      6 lira notes
Doors down R, closed
Doors up C, open
Windows closed
Window curtains open
Table-lamp C, out
Fire out
Candelabra, out

*Off stage:*  Kate's handbag (SUSAN)

*Personal:*  SUSAN: handbag
          MAUD: handbag

## SCENE 2

*Set:*  Small table (below wing-chair) *On it:* lace cloth, silver tray with tea
      in silver pot, milk in silver jug, silver bowl of lump sugar with
      tongs, 2 cups, 2 saucers, 2 teaspoons, slop basin, 2 small plates
      Tiered cake-stand (L of wing-chair) *On it:* lace cloths on each tier,
      plate of cakes and cut cake
      *On R end of desk:* box of matches, oil-lamp
Move stool down R to R of table below wing-chair
Doors closed
Window curtains open

Fire lit
Fittings out

*Off stage:*  Lighted oil-lamp (GANASETA)
              2 lighted oil-lamps (MARIA)
              Salver. *On it:* visiting card (GANASETA)


# ACT III

## SCENE 1

*Strike:*  All oil-lamps
Reset stool down R

*Set:*  Unlit oil-lamp (on desk)
        Unlit oil-lamp (on table R of doors up C)
        *On mantelpiece:* box of matches
Doors shut
Window curtains open
Fire out
Fittings out

*Off stage:*  Oil-lamp, lit (PASQUALE)
              Oil-lamp, lit (SUSAN)

*Personal:*  MILLY: shawl
             SUSAN: handkerchief


## SCENE 2

*Strike:*  Oil-lamps
           Stationery from desk

*Set:*  *On table* C: oil-lamp, unlit
Windows closed
Curtains open
Fittings out
Fire lit
Door down L open
Doors up C, shut

*Off stage:*  Large sealed envelope. *In it:* Lawyer's letter with lists of Milly's
              assets (MERTON)
              Small sealed letter (MERTON)

# LIGHTING PLOT

Property fittings required : 3 tall, ornate, six-branch standard candelabra,
each with 6 tall candles and shades
5 oil-lamps
Fire-grate (coal)

Interior. A Venetian salon. The same scene throughout

The Main Acting Areas are at a chaise-longue RC, at a wing-chair C, at a desk LC and at two windows L
The Apparent Sources of Light are, in daytime, tall, french windows L; and at night, by candelabra and oil-lamps as directed

ACT I, Scene 1. An October afternoon

*To open :*    Effect of sunshine
Fire out
1 oil-lamp C, out
Other fittings off stage
*No cues*

ACT I, Scene 2. Evening

*To open :*    Standard candelabrum with 6 candles lit (L of doors up C)
Standard candelabrum with 3 candles lit (R of fireplace)
Oil-lamp on table C, lit
Oil-lamp on table L, lit
Fire out
Dark outside windows

*Cue* 1     Ganaseta lights 3 candles                (Page 19)
*Bring in 3 unlit candles on candelabrum R of fireplace*

*Cue* 2     Ganaseta enters up C with oil lamp         (Page 23)
*Increase general lighting*

*Cue* 3     Ganaseta enters up C with second oil lamp      (Page 23)
*Increase general lighting still further*

ACT II, Scene 1. Morning

*To open:* Effect of sunshine
Fire out
Fittings out
*No cues*

ACT II, Scene 2. Afternoon

*To open:* Effect of sunset
Fire lit
Fittings out

*Cue* 4    After rise of Curtain      (Page 42)
*Commence slow dim of lights for twilight effect*

*Cue* 5    Merton lights lamp      (Page 43)
*Bring up lights a little* c

*Cue* 6    Ganaseta and Maria enter with lamps      (Page 45)
*Bring up general lighting*

ACT III, Scene 1. Evening

*To open:* The stage dim, the only light coming from the windows
The night sky murky
Fire out
Oil-lamp on desk, out
Oil-lamp on table R of doors up C, out

*Cue* 7    Pasquale and Susan enter with lamps      (Page 51)
*Bring up lights up* c

*Cue* 8    Pasquale lights fire      (Page 51)
*Bring in fire glow*

*Cue* 9    Susan lights lamp on desk      (Page 52)
*Bring up lights* lc

ACT III, Scene 2. Afternoon

*To open:* Effect of clear daylight
Fire lit
Fittings out
*No cues*